UNSLICED

UNSLICED

HOW TO STAY WHOLE IN THE PIZZERIA INDUSTRY

MIKE BAUSCH

LIONCREST
PUBLISHING

UNSLICED
How to Stay Whole in the Pizzeria Industry

ISBN   978-1-5445-1665-3   *Hardcover*
978-1-5445-1666-0   *Paperback*
978-1-5445-1664-6   *Ebook*
978-1-5445-1742-1   *Audiobook*

Dedications don't make sense to me.

It's like when people give out song dedications; it's not like you wrote the song. The DJ is just playing it. In this case, I wrote it. I did so for the people reading it, so they could read it and benefit. Soooooooo...

This book is dedicated to you.
Yes, you. The one with the book in your hand.

*This is for you, for the days you think
no one else has been through it;
you now know you are not alone and
you can get through it and kill it.*

*Dedications are really more like grandiose
thank yous: Here are my grandiose, appropriate, and well-deserved thank yous:*

*I'd like to truly thank my amazing Wife, Michelle.
She's solid, caring, pushes in her work as hard*

as I try to, and is a constant inspiration. Also, my Son Henry who makes this all worth it.

My Mom, Marge, who would have loved to see this, and who would have looked at the book and said, "It's a very nice book, honey...oh, but I don't like the photo you chose of yourself."

My brother and business partner, Jim, who made this all a possibility and who worked with me for all this time to formulate the content you will read here.

My father, Lt. Col. Arthur Bausch, who has lived his life leading by example. My Dad is the kindest and smartest leader I have ever known, and I'm lucky to have him.

With love to my sisters, Eileen and Laurie, who have always sought to watch out for me. Also love to all of my nieces, nephews, and extended family. Especially, Danny.

*Also:
All of my staff present and past, most especially Alfredo Herrera.*

Special thank you to Mandy Vavrinak, who knew our story needed to be told before anyone else. As well as Lisa Riley and Meagan Duvall, who help spread our message.

The City of Tulsa, where the American Dream still thrives. It's still the best-kept secret in the US, and the place I call home after many homes before.

Kathy Taylor, Elizabeth Frame Ellison, and the whole Lobeck-Taylor Foundation.

Special thanks to Gil Eacret of Security Bank, who gave us a loan and believed in our vision, when every other bank said no.

Daphne Dinsmore, RN, who has treated me like family and helped me get through my tough times with type 1 diabetes.

My extended pizza family at Pizza Today Magazine; *Bill Oakley, Pete La Chapelle, Jeremy White, Josh Keown, and Denise Greer.*

Performance Foodservice/Roma Foods, who has been a constant partner. Namely Fred Dallas, Stephen Piancone, Fred Sanelli, Joe Davi, Gulio Binetti, Karen Marshall, Mark Duffy, Susan Highly, Dustin Bishop, and my first Roma Rep, Eric Burns. Also, our sponsors and supporters over the years with Big Tray, Shawnee

*Mills, Alex Manzo & Manzo Foods, Rotoflex,
Artisan Pizza Solutions, and Stainislaus Foods.*

*Especially Tony Gemignani, for being my sage
guide and friend. Thank you, Tony, for taking a
call from a dumbass twenty-two-year-old in 2005.*

*Also my pizza friends, namely Jeff Smokevitch, Scott
Anthony, Siler Chapman, Michael Shepard, Ken
Bryant, Sean Brauser, Joe Carlucci, Glenn Cybulski,
Tony "Mr. Gorgeous" Troiano, Carmine Testa and his
sons Michael and Nicholas, Will Grant, Nick Bogacz,
John Arena, Nicole Bean, Massimiliano Saieva, Tara
Hattan, Laura Meyer, and every member of the World
Pizza Champions including Thomas Schneider,
Derek Sanchez, Justin Wadstein, Matt Driscoll, Mitch
Rotolo, Paul Cataldo, Thiago Vasconcelos, Frank
Baird, Tony Cerimele, Anthony Scardino, Billy Manzo,
Giovanni Cesarno, David Whisker, Eric Von Hansen,
Shawn Randazzo, Matt Molina, Pete Tolman,
Michael Mercurio, Audrey Kelly, Brittany Saxton,
Leo Spizzirri, Melissa Rickman, and Joseph Mercurio.
With love to Willy O and Big Dave and their families.*

*To everyone at KMOD, especially Corbin and
Biggie Shay for touting us on-air when we were
just one store in Owasso. And Genny Cram, Sam,
and Michael "Gimpy" Berger at KMOD, too.*

Tucker Max, Jane Borden, Hal Clifford,
and the entire Scribe Team.

The inspirational kindness, ingenuity, and lead-
ership of Chris Bianco. The thoughtful resil-
ience of Mick Foley to always get back up, and
the grit and motivation I still hear yelling in my
ear of Sergeant Major Jean-Paul Courville.

To anyone else along the way, where if you made
me laugh or helped me out or if we crossed paths
in any way meaningful enough that you decided
to read my book, then I am sincerely grate-
ful. Especially all my teachers and coaches and
friends in the YMCA, De La Salle High School, St.
Mary's College of California, and Vic Stewart's.

Paolo, Kurt, Andy, Brendan, Kenny, John,
Jon, Mike, Eric, Jeremy, Nate, and A.J.

Also to _____,
whom I can't believe I almost forgot.

This book is in no way, shape, or form dedicated
to Lou Diamond Phillips. Absolutely not. If you
hear him take credit for this in any way, know now
I do not vouch or endorse Mr. Phillips and have

no intention of doing so in the future. If you are reading this, Lou, stop now, nothing in this book will help you or your cause. You don't even own a restaurant business, Lou, so I don't know why you're still reading. It's not for you, man, move on.

CONTENTS

Foreword   **xiii**

1. This is Your Warning   **1**
2. Get Your Mind Right   **11**
3. The Impressive Experience   **27**
4. Why Should Anyone Buy from You?   **43**
5. Why Should Anyone Work for You?   **65**
6. Communication to Staff   **109**
7. Do I Suck? And Why "Yes" Is a Great Answer   **143**
8. Create Million Dollar Systems   **157**
9. How to Win with People Not on Your Payroll   **189**
10. So, You're the Shit Now?   **223**
11. Owning Ownership   **251**

Conclusion: Staying Relevant   **267**

Unsliced Restaurant Terms Glossary   **281**
About the Author   **285**

FOREWORD

Monday, March 16th, 2020

The rumors of what we heard over the weekend are true. This is about to play out, and we will have to close stores. What's happening on the coasts is about to happen here in Tulsa. Tomorrow, because of COVID-19, the city will pull the plug on dine-in, and we will need to be able to figure this shit out quick.

Fifteen-plus years have all led to this. Have to dig deep in the bag of tricks. Lives are on the line. The economy's at play and the public's safety is at the forefront. Everyone's looking to you for what the fuck we're about to do with all this.

I know we're going to have to furlough about half the employees at a minimum. That also means we're going to need to close the stores that are predicated upon communal dining. The gelaterias and our fine-dining restaurant, Prossimo, will have to close.

OK, ten- second-gut-check time, Bausch.

Are we going to get through this?

Are we prepared to take this on?

Am I game to figure it out if we aren't?

Ten seconds gone. Yep, I want this, and we're game. It's time to nut the fuck up and make shit happen. Our managers and hourly workers need cash. All the furloughed workers need you to dig in on this one so they can come back to work when it's safe to do so.

I don't believe we'll live in a world where restaurants don't exist. Without restaurants, what's the point of living. What's the point of working your ass off, if not to have great food around the people you love? I also don't believe in any scenario where Tulsa doesn't have Andolini's as a part of its scene.

Reliance on the skillset is what will get us through this.

It's time to get smart and utilize the relationships that we've cultivated and nurtured for more than fifteen years. It's time to talk to other restaurant owners and get a feel for what they're planning. Then I need to get with other pizzeria owners from states already affected by these closures. These people are my friends, and I need to know what they're dealing with, so I'm better educated to make my own decision.

I don't know how this government-proposed SBA money thing is going to work, but our finances are in order. We're not a dirty pirate ship bullshitting our way through this business. Having tight books and a clean record will pay off. I believe our bank will help get us through this. They trust us, and we trust them.

Tuesday, March 17th, 2020

This will be the shittiest St Patrick's Day ever. Fiscally, it will be a bloodbath, and what should be a packed party in Tulsa will instead be a ghost town with empty streets. It wouldn't matter if St. Patrick himself drove out the snakes today, since there's no one on the streets to care.

The week was already off to a shit start. Why wouldn't it be, when everyone is freaked out about everything. Customers are scared, not knowing if they might be losing their jobs. Kids are being told to stay at home, and parents aren't ready to take on the responsibility of becoming teachers overnight.

We've furloughed as few people as possible. How the hell did the word furlough become a commonly used word in my professional vocabulary?

Cutting off half our labor costs won't be enough. We'll still need to get to 60% of our standard run rate of sales to afford payroll. If we don't do that, we'll have issues paying our monthly state sales tax that's due Friday.

Wednesday, March 18th, 2020

The only way to get by is to find another angle. We need an amazingly strong weekend in sales with no dine-in and a curbside business model we've never tried before. It's time to throw it all at the wall and see what sticks.

You've executed a serious pivot before. Now just do it all again, except this time do it all in one day.

What's the angle, what do people need? This is an opportunity; this is a confined audience. What do they need? Time to try a pizza kit for parents to make with their kids. Never did it before out of fear of cannibalizing sales, but that's out the window. Need a photo of the kit, an email blast, a recipe guide for staff, and customer instructions for the kit made, and then sent out for staff to print, and I have about an hour to pull that off before going to the bank to handle SBA items.

I need to make a Facebook video advertising a corporate-catering service we can push through our food truck. Pretty videos aren't an option; this is purely hit play and go. We'll need another email blast and Instagram post about it as well.

We need to help out staff stuck at home someway. If we push gift card sales, it will give us a cash injection to the business, and then we can provide staff 20% of whatever we sell in gift cards. We can feed them slices before lunch and dinner rush. We can have Prossimo chefs turn their unused product into pantry items for staff to take home. They can make soups, sauces, and anything else they can dream up out of what we have. That way, families have food during this.

I have to keep their morale up. We need to use our notification system to provide our (nearly three hundred) employees with a rundown of the situation in depth. They'll need to know how to file for furlough pay, which is really unemployment, but I can't even stomach saying the word aloud. We've worked our balls off for fifteen years to employ as many people as possible, and here I am sending them on fucking unemployment. I can't change COVID, but what I can do is right this ship and get us back on course.

Basic Leadership Plan time (chapter five) assess, develop, execute, and communicate. Need revenue bad, so create every promo we can, execute them all, and then pursue further the ones that work.

Are big-name companies going to use us for catering? I sure hope so. Are we going to have random people coming out of the woodwork to buy gift cards? I don't know, but we're going to try every single thing, knowing at least some things will work.

Safety evaluation. No one has masks, but we can use bandanas and get by on those. I need to call up my doctor friends and ask their opinion of what our staff should do during this to stay safe. I'll see if any can come on-site and do a site eval.

Thursday, March 19th, 2020

We've done two marketing emails, and I've done a video every day on Facebook and pushed it on Instagram. The idea of doing a pizza kit is resonating, but no one is calling us up about the food truck. No corporations are allowing anyone from off-site onto their premises. Have to get my truck guys a gig, or I will have to furlough them as well. Maybe we can send the truck into a neighborhood and see if people just want to leave their homes and get a slice of pizza. Can't hurt to try it and see if we at least break even.

My friend, who works at the hospital, is coming by to evaluate our set up. She says their protocol is to keep a log of employees' temperatures and to sanitize shoes and items upon entry, and that we should do the same. Easy enough, I wouldn't have thought to do it otherwise, but this way, we maintain safety. No one else is doing this yet, but if it's safer, we're doing it.

Friday, March 20th, 2020

Staff is eating from the pantry, and we're doing good on gift card sales so we can help out people who request funds. We have an obligation to our workforce to help them through this with us. A failure point is our phone system. They're going to be used way more than usual. We need to figure out a redundant back up when the lines jam. I've hoped for luck in the past during times like this. Fuck hope; we need to pull this off. I'll make pizzas in our Andolini's Broken Arrow store, then head to my Jenks location. After I know they're set, I'll head into Tulsa proper and hit up Andolini's on Cherry Street.

Saturday, March 21st, 2020

Food truck test run in the neighborhood. You gotta be shitting me. The same truck I couldn't beg a business to take? It just did five times its typical Saturday sales by 3 p.m. They have a line fifty people deep going one hundred yards. All the customers are socially distancing themselves without my truck guys needing to tell them. We're going to need more flour, pepperoni, and mozzarella from Roma Foodservice on the fly, or we're going to run out. Don't know how that became a problem of this shitty week, but I'll happily take it.

Sunday, March 22nd, 2020

No Roma truck drivers on Sunday, so the head of business development, Mark Duffy, is driving the shipment down. Love that guy. It's a three-and-a-half-hour drive from Springfield, Missouri, to Tulsa, so I'll meet the truck then set up getting the product to each individual store.

The staff that got furloughed this week is understanding of the situation and we have them set up in the system for unemployment. The staff that's working is tired, but morale is up. Anxiety has softened, and somehow, we're cracking jokes and having fun. It looks like we can add twenty more staff members to payroll and reduce the furlough group.

Monday, March 23rd, 2020

We made it. We're going to be able to pay payroll, and our taxes are set. We hit our goals. We sold over 1,500 pizza kits and have the food truck booked for lunch and dinner for the next three weeks. It's not enough to fix all this, but we will get through this; after this week, I know we will get through this.

During all this, we simultaneously got our paperwork set for the SBA. We're prepared for the next hurdle, and we've played this thing smart so far. I know another hurdle's coming. I know there's going to be discrepancies and failure points. Regardless, we pivoted from losing all of our dine-in business to offering only curbside service and we mitigated this nightmare.

This world will still have our pizzeria next month, next year, and for the foreseeable future. They will still have it because of the skillset we've acquired over the past fifteen years. The skills detailed in this book. Better relations, employee morale, mindset, marketing, and dedication. We will learn from this and come out of it with new techniques and ingenuity to get us through the next era of business. This, I know.

That was my mindset in the hardest week in the history of the restaurant industry. By the following Friday, I was asked by *Fox & Friends* to speak nationally on a Skype call filmed live on my cell phone. I shot it in my kitchen early in the morning, using the Tulsa flag as the backdrop. I detailed what this closure meant to restaurants and how we were going to get through it. I talked about how hard things had been and about how much harder they might get, so the general public could be aware. I did this interview, so the regular consumer knew, from me to them, that restaurants, as a whole, are in danger. The way we got through it wasn't by putting our head down and hoping for the best. It was by demanding the best from ourselves and forcing our way through the shit storm.

I've had a lot of bad days and a lot of great days running a restaurant. I've never had every single aspect of the restaurant tested simultaneously in such a short amount of time. I've had the sprinkler pop on a Friday night rush. I've had our gelato van t-boned by a criminal evading the police in a high-speed chase. I've had employees I cared about die because of cancer or alcoholism and I've sent some of the people closest with me to rehab. I've been through fights with my brother over the restaurant. I've felt chewed up and beaten down only to lay it all on the line. And I've done this multiple times, every time hoping something would come to fruition. I'm fucking done with hope. It's now about knowledge and embracing systems and strategies that yield results. After fifteen years of agita, fuckups, and triumph, this is that result.

On days when everything goes to shit, I think of USMC General Chesty Puller. He said this in the Korean

War battle of the Chosin Reservoir: "We're surrounded. That simplifies the problem." When you can handle your operational worst and still rebound, it makes you better; it builds confidence.

COVID was not my rock bottom. It was another hard thing that necessitated the creation of a new system to deal with it. My worst times were before the systems. This last week, as I am writing this book, I had a day where my water got shut off at 5 p.m. right before dinner due to a line break, forcing two of my restaurants out of operation. That same day, I fired a GM (General Manager) and had to mitigate an unrelated potential PR nightmare on Facebook. What would have been debilitating before is now just SOP (Standard Operating Procedure). I'm able to handle the crazy with systems—systems that expect the unexpected.

WHY WE'RE HERE

I can teach you how to build systems that not only handle the crazy but create sales and sanity. It's on you to pick yourself back up when you fall, but I will teach you how to stand taller when you do. Through self-reliance, smart systems, and solid hard work, you will be better. These systems and protocols will protect you and your restaurant.

If you own a pizzeria or restaurant, you're probably struggling with food cost. You wonder how to get customers to come back more often. It drives you nuts just getting employees to do what they're supposed to do—their job.

I want *you* to know that I know *you* already. You own or are about to own a pizzeria or restaurant. You're scared shitless sometimes but don't want to let others know how scared you are. You even are trying to hide from yourself how scared you get. You think you are on the right path, but you aren't sure. This restaurant thing is overwhelming, and it feels like you're in a 110-degree car and need to roll down the window, but you don't know how to or simply can't.

That's because the pizza business is more cutthroat, stressful, and multi-faceted than working on Wall Street. I know my Wall Street friends want nothing to do with my gig. No one is giving you the blueprint or process to get traction. You just want to make some pizzas, be happy, do what you love, make money, and have the world thank you for it. Instead, the opposite of that seems to be your reality.

I can help you.

I want to help you.

By the way, I have a predisposition to immediately not trust anyone who "wants" to help me. I want to help you because I don't want to see you or anyone suffer through this. This industry is brutally harsh, and *it doesn't have to be*. I will teach you how to get out of your own way and not be an employee but a boss. I will show you how to keep your business thriving for a lifetime, or however long you wish to do this for.

When I figure something out I don't like to hide it; I'm proud of it and think, "Oh, well look at this, that shit worked. Hey guys, come over here and check out this shit that works." If I can help, I will. That's the Irish-Italian Catholic in me. I feel insurmountable guilt for every wasted opportunity to not make things better. That is who I am.

What I am not is a bullshit artist or snake oil salesman. I'm not theorizing this; I'm living this. What I share is a tried and true practical method I have learned from failures. The failures that I hope you can avoid.

My restaurant, Andolini's Pizzeria, was named one of the "Top 10 Pizzerias in America" based solely on reviews by TripAdvisor, CNN, Buzzfeed, and *USA Today*. Business.org named Tulsa as one of the most food-obsessed cities in the United States, with Andolini's as the "most recommended restaurant" in Tulsa. This city has more restaurants per person than Miami, Dallas, and NYC, and there are more hits than misses in Tulsa.

I'm a Certified Master Pizzaiolo and instructor. I've won Tulsa's Restaurateur of the Year, and my restaurant regularly wins "best of" in Tulsa, Oklahoma, and other national accolades. Andolini's makes Tulsa Style pizza. I call it that because it isn't New York style and it isn't California style. Andolini's pizza style is a mix of New York fermentation practices and California ingenuity.

And it's unique because we use Oklahoma flour. In other words, it's Tulsa style. (We also serve Napoletana and Romana styles, and use the appropriate Italian flour for each.)

My restaurants have bars and a robust full menu that does massive catering orders. In the fifteen years since I started Andolini's with my brother Jim, our restaurant company has grown to five brick-and-mortar Andolini's locations, a food truck, two gelaterias, two food hall concepts, and a fine dining Italian restaurant: Prossimo Ristorante. Prossimo was named one of the *Best New Restaurants of 2019* with a five-star review by *Tulsa World*. My brother and I own and operate all of our locations with no outside investors or franchising.

The methodology we use comes from a simple nuts-and-bolts work ethic molded by discipline and leadership traits we learned in the Marine Corps. My father is a Retired Lieutenant Colonel who fought in Vietnam and helped mold the Marine Corps image over his twenty-two year tenure. My brother was a Marine UH-1 "Huey" helicopter crew chief in the '80s, and I was in USMC OCS (Officer Candidate School) in the summer of 2002. My Marine Corps journey ended abruptly when I learned I was a type 1 juvenile diabetic. At age twenty, my Marine Corps path was done. I held down OCS training as a 135-pound, frail weakling with no fat or muscle in my body after being ravaged by a slow churning diabetic breakdown. I didn't realize what was occurring over those two years, all culminating in a three-day hospital stay five days after returning from OCS. I never went to sickbay in Quantico, Virginia, during training. This taught me that I'm a stubborn fuck when I want something to be a reality. Even if my body disagrees, my mind will win. That trial by fire made opening a restaurant at twenty-two with minimal restaurant experience possible. I am now a functioning insulin-dependent type 1 diabetic. Having one summer in Quantico does not compare to the service of my father, brother, and every other service member out there. It provided an example of the structure, discipline, and ethos I could apply to my alternate path of owning a restaurant.

(Diabetic note: type 1 diabetes is the diabetes you can't fix by taking a pill and being healthier and more active. One day your pancreas says, "I'm out, YO. Catch you later, Brah," and never comes back to the party. It happens to kids three to twenty-nine on average and is called juvenile diabetes. Think of Mary Tyler Moore or Bret Michaels. Type 2 diabetes is AKA the Wilford Brimley "Dia-Bettus," and is hereditary to a degree, but a bad lifestyle, obesity, and age all factor into it. Like, think Paula Dean and Tracy Morgan.)

This book is purposefully unlike any other pizza or pizza marketing book out there. There are pizza recipe books, there are books about getting your store open, and they should all be read by you if you're looking to be better. Michael Shepard's book *Growing Pizza* is an excellent read. Scott Anthony's *Profits in the Pie*, along with Nick Bogacz's *The Pizza Equation*, have incredibly astute takes on the industry.

This book is about mindset. This is about functional system creation. If you want a book of great recipes for making pizza and Italian dishes, *Bianco: Pizza, Pasta, and Other Food I Like* by Chris Bianco is superb. If you want a comprehensive look at how to make every type of pizza, then your go-to book is *The Pizza Bible* by Tony Gemignani. For the home chef or restauranteur, Tony Gemignani's book is a mic drop for all things pizza.

Odds are you're comfortable, maybe even prideful, about your pizza skills.

This book is for everything else that goes along with this industry. To the person who's barely making rent and doesn't know why things aren't clicking: this book is for you.

If any of this sounds familiar, or if there's any aspect of your business you're not satisfied with, then I have one question for you:

What are you going to do about it?

A. Whine 'til your restaurant closes and point fingers after the fact, *or...*
B. Decide your own fate, nut-up, and unfuck your existence

FOR THIS AUDITORY PALATE CLEANSER

Consider this first one an amuse-bouche for this literary journey. Between chapters, I will suggest a reflective or applicable song, or experience. For these cleansers, stream, download, or do whatever people do to enjoy music.

How do you pay your staff and charities, get accolades, and run a business? The answer always comes back to cash flow. This isn't a book on accounting; it's a book on making smart moves that get you paid.

From 36 Chambers, this song from the Shaolin is self-explanatory. For when shit gets raw, and it's time to hustle, use this song.

Please enjoy,

"C.R.E.A.M."
by Wu-Tang Clan

CHAPTER 1

THIS IS YOUR WARNING

D o you choose the red pill or the blue pill? In the film *The Matrix*, choosing the unglamorous truth meant choosing the red pill. Choosing the blue pill meant living in blissful ignorance. This chapter is the red pill chapter, where I tell you this will super suck. I mean this job is a cavalcade of continuous kicks to the balls. This life is an onslaught of suckitude to get to a life of non-suckitude. To avoid or at least endure less of that suckitude, you need to *actually read this book*. I realize that sounds obvious, but if you only skim this book, you will not make your restaurant better, and the purchase will have been useless.

However, if you do actually read this book, I guarantee it will help you. You need to decide right now for this book and for your restaurant which statement you relate to more:

A. I am a person who tries hard, and the effort is what counts.

Orrrrrrrrrrrrr

B. I like setting my mind to things and then actually accomplishing them. I love the process along the way of making something happen.

If you choose B, then you are results-driven, and you "Embrace the Suck." This means, when shit gets gnarly, you dig finding a way out of it. I'm pretty sure that personality trait isn't necessarily normal or healthy, i.e., to be a glutton for punishment. However, it is an essential trait of anyone looking to own their own business—especially a pizzeria.

If you signed on to owning your own restaurant hoping to become a celebrity chef or because you just don't like your job and think owning a restaurant will be "fun," then do not pass go, do not collect two hundred dollars. Instead, wrap that shit up, call it a day, take a vacay, talk to a therapist, or find a headhunter and adjust your current worldview because...

A restaurant is not the answer to your existing problems. It's asking for a shitload of new problems.

The amount of work it takes to not only survive but also make an impact with a restaurant is massive. A restaurant that lasts for years takes absolute humility. You must acknowledge daily how much you suck at restauranting, until one day you don't suck anymore. That is a lot for the average person to absorb. The restaurant life *will* affect your home life drastically. Restaurants destroy relationships and consume your mental health and quality of life. This life choice is 100% a gamble.

A gamble you might succeed in, in your hope to serve people food in an industry with a meager financial return rate and an extremely high failure rate. If you haven't committed to a restaurant yet, please pause and ask yourself this question: do you need this?

You: "I *need* this; I need to own a restaurant. I don't just want to own a restaurant, I absolutely *fucking NEED* to do this. This is my calling; this is my shit. I got this, and nothing else will suffice."

If that statement sounded stupid as you said it out loud, then restaurant-ownership isn't for you.

That last statement was not a challenge from me to you. This is all about being real with yourself. I can't walk into a law firm and say, "I'd like to do civil court litigation, do you have any openings? I've seen a shit-ton of *Law & Order*, so yeah, *I got this*." That's an outrageous notion. However, lots of failed restaurants started with the mindset of: "I've eaten at a ton of nice restaurants. I'm a great cook, and I'm going to start a restaurant." You can't be an opera singer after killing it on karaoke night at the Slippery Whistle, and you can't be a tech mogul because you're the shit at Words with Friends.

If you have never even operated or worked in a restaurant, then don't assume for a second that you know anything. Instead, your best move is to concede you know nothing so you can be a blank canvas ready for paint.

DECIDING TO START A PIZZERIA

But Mike, did you always know that you wanted to own a pizza shop? For me, the answer is no. Don't get me wrong. *I love pizza*, and so do you; so does everyone. Anyone who doesn't love pizza is a garbage individual who should roll themselves up in a carpet, like the trash sushi they are, and commit an act of Bushido. All this should be done in an effort to rid their family of the dishonor they bring upon their kin's name when they conversationally say, "I'm not into pizza. I don't know why, I just don't like pizza."

Loving pizza doesn't make you special. Loving it from a young age doesn't qualify one to own a pizzeria. If that were the case, Charles Edward Cheese, DBA

Chuck E. Cheese, would be producing a long line of pizzeria owners.

To succeed in a restaurant takes a lot of failures, a lot of trials and tribulations, a lot of eating crow, for very little thanks. You will never take a bow in front of an audience. You will never get a standing ovation after a hard night of work on the pizza line. If you're lucky, one day, you might get an award, and you might have a few people that acknowledge it. That's the best case in terms of accolades and appreciation for your efforts. The subtle joy of seeing a kid ask their parents to go to your pizzeria, a date night choosing your pizzeria, or a graduation party choosing your pizzeria to enjoy their special moment is as good as it gets. Don't get me wrong, that's pretty good if you're into that type of thing, which I am.

What's in it for you, then? What you could achieve here is a lasting contribution to your local culture. You can have the knowledge that no one owns you. You probably won't get a mansion, or five-star vacations, or yachts, or new Corvettes—maybe a convertible, but it will be a Mazda Miata before it's a Corvette. You won't have the corner office, but did you really want that? You'll miss out on a bunch of '90s furniture with motivational posters or worse, landscape paintings from Hobby Lobby on the wall as you listen to the Muzak version of MacArthur Park on your walk to the drinking fountain in a JoS. A. Bank suit that doesn't fit right.

Did you want to wait in line to eat lunch at the corporate café or bring your lunch to work in a baggie like a fifth grader, or do you prefer making your own lunch in your kitchen? Do you want to drive that nice car in bumper-to-bumper traffic at 5 p.m., or tired as shit after working for yourself at 11 p.m. with no one on the road? Maybe it's me, but when I think of the 9 to 5 world, I get the heebie-jeebies. All I can hear is Ray Liotta's line from Goodfellas, that 9 to 5 people are saps, dead already, no balls. (I legally can't quote it verbatim, but it's at the 17:45 mark in the film.)

So, for all my warnings, I will say this; this job is pretty cool. When Cubicle Gary dies, only his immediate family will notice because corporate cog life doesn't contribute to the culture. That's not the case for restaurant owners. If affecting culture and making an impact gives you the yawns, then once more, this isn't for you. It's not going to work out because you don't care about impact, your priorities lie elsewhere, and *that is fine*; do something else.

The restaurant and pizza industry is not filled with Fyrefest and Theranos CEOs bullshitting their way to the top. It is impossible in this industry to fake it 'til you make it, or in their case, fake it 'til you fail it. You fail at the beginning. You get fired or you close. If you're really, really good at making pizza, and you think you have an amazing pizza recipe, then *goooood for yooooouuuu*.

I want you to know that I said that just as it was written, extremely facetiously. Good for you because it doesn't matter. Why? Great food is only the price of entry. The HR, the marketing, the sheer agility, and the marathon it takes to run a restaurant will destroy your love of pizza-making unless it's hard-coded into your brain.

After fifteen years of this, I know now that I should have failed. I should have failed multiple times. Here's why I and WE didn't. Because when everything falls to complete shit, I don't. I nut up, and I say, "OK, world, let's do this." I am not a genius; I am not God's gift to pizza-making. I'm just a guy who doesn't like to fail out of spite, and my brother and business partner Jim is the same way. If you're stupid for this industry like we are, welcome aboard, let's get to work.

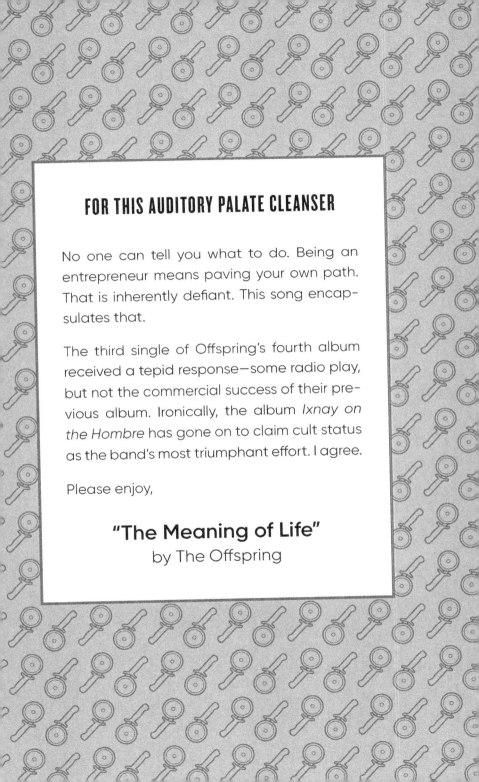

FOR THIS AUDITORY PALATE CLEANSER

No one can tell you what to do. Being an entrepreneur means paving your own path. That is inherently defiant. This song encapsulates that.

The third single of Offspring's fourth album received a tepid response—some radio play, but not the commercial success of their previous album. Ironically, the album *Ixnay on the Hombre* has gone on to claim cult status as the band's most triumphant effort. I agree.

Please enjoy,

"The Meaning of Life"
by The Offspring

CHAPTER 2

GET YOUR MIND RIGHT

W hen I saw *Cool Hand Luke* as a kid, I instantly resonated with it. If you haven't seen it, I highly suggest you do, and watch it like a film, with no distractions in a dark room. There is a scene in the film where Luke and the chain gang need to pave a seemingly endless tar road. It should take them late into the night to finish, in grueling heat. Luke rallies all the inmates to get done faster to stick it to the guards who rely on their broken docile spirit to remain that way. Luke pushes everyone with upbeat morale and, as a team, they get it done before sunset. They're left with nothing to do but enjoy the view as the guards look on bewildered. With enthusiasm for the day, fortitude, and genuine motivation, you can achieve the impossible. It is your job to replicate that spirit every day in your business.

Having an unbroken spirit is necessary for you to succeed. Your mind needs to be stubborn, not stupid, but stubborn. I want you to know right now; you are not special. Once you know that you aren't special, you can make moves, strategic moves needed to thrive. You are only as valuable as the opportunities you create and the ones you take advantage of. Your mind must be geared towards resolve and not excuses. Your mind must say, "I got it," not, "Whose job is this?" You must be a doer and not don't-er. *I cannot teach you this*; it's a choice every day you make not to suck or at least to suck less. Along with stubbornness, will-to-win confidence is vital. Luke is ordinary, but he is courageous; never cocky but very confident: be like Luke.

CONFIDENCE VS. COCKINESS

You've heard my warnings, and you know for sure that this life is for you. You have chosen to do this. No other path is worth it for you. I applaud you. Your ego is deflated and your motivation is inflated. Your mind is right, and you're ready to Get Shit Done (GSD). The hallmarks of a successful entrepreneur are what you possess.

If you aren't open already, the first day will be a far cry from where you end up. Staff will change, menus will evolve, and that's OK. If your store is the same as it was day one, then you aren't progressing, and nobody gets it perfect on their first day.

On the opening day of the first Andolini's, we woke up super early and made the dough that day. That's a rookie error out the gate. If you know dough, you know it's dumb to make dough the day that you're planning to sell it and not give it time to proof. We thought, "No one will come in on our first day; it should be fine." We got annihilated, or so we thought. The entire business we did that first day, we do by noon nowadays, but at the time, it was a lot to take on.

I wasn't a pizzaiolo when I opened Andolini's. My brother and I had worked pizza places, but the level of pizzeria we had worked at wasn't culinarily astounding. That didn't matter, though, because both of us were highly dedicated to putting our egos aside and making this thing real. I said, "I didn't drive halfway across America and give up law school to suck at making pizza."

With all that said, on the drive to open up the restaurant on the first day, we said a few stupid things. One of the first crazy things was, "We'll get this Andolini's open, have another one set to open in about six months. By two years from now, we'll be running around four restaurants." That did not happen. We didn't open our second restaurant until six years after our first, and that was precisely when it should have been. Store one is super hard, store two is just as hard, and if you rush store two, the whole thing falls apart.

That's cool. That's the way it should be. You need to get it right before you move on to more. Everything needs to be perfect, running on its own for weeks before you consider leaving it for another venture. I will talk more on store two troubles later, but remember this, you *can't* play two instruments at once well. You *can*, however, be a maestro to multiple instruments. If you are playing the harpsichord, you better be able to teach someone how to do it as well as you before you go on to the oboe.

The very confident statement we made that first day, that I advise you say to yourself, was this: "I'm smart, and all these other dummies figured this pizza thing out, so how can we not be able to figure this out?" That is confidence. While I advise against being a cocky bastard, you must be confident.

I highly suggest confidence. I thoroughly denounce being cocky or egotistical.

Confident: I can do this.
Cocky: I can do this in my sleep, and it will be super easy.
Egotistical: Without much effort, I will be, or already am, the best person to have ever done this.

For every task you become confident in, you must train others to do as well. Then you should do something new and avoid the complacency of doing what you are comfortable doing, i.e., learn to delegate.

You need to know what jobs are for you and what jobs are not for you. Every job is for you until you either decide that you aren't that good at it or that you've mastered it and it has become not worth your limited time. Ideally, you learn how to get better at and master every task before you delegate it to other people.

FIND YOUR VOICE

The first few years of a restaurant are a lot like a stand-up comic's first few years developing their act and learning their voice. Anyone can get some laughs around their friends, but to be a real comic means people pay you to be funny. Just like people pay restaurants for food. You must have quality funny to be a lasting comic with a unique act, and you must have a fantastic restaurant experience to last as a restaurant owner. No comic goes on stage day one and is ready to sell out Madison Square Garden, let alone a paying room of thirty people. They typically work for free or close to it. Even a funny comedian takes years to become special, years to be the performer that stands out from the rest. The same goes for restaurants. You can serve people and be good. To last, you have to be different. To be a great restaurant means you find your voice and brand identity.

The big difference between day one of a pizzeria and day one of a comic's career is a comic doesn't have their financial ass on the line. You don't have the economic benefit of kicking the can down the road to see what happens. Odds are a lot of money is on the line and food cost and payroll costs are only compounding the issue. You're expected to do something worthy of payment on the first day of business, and that's a big ask. The only way out is through trial and error to improve and enough fuck-up money to sustain the valley.

In the time you are learning your "voice," or in this case, defining your brand, you will need to nail down questions like these:

- Is my restaurant the high-end choice for pizza?
- Are we the kitschy fun brand for families?
- Is our business model based on proximity, for example, the go-to pizza choice in a young college town?
- Is this the date night pizzeria, the game-day pizzeria, or neither?

You most likely have considered these questions. Maybe you locked in on one. However, be prepared for life to beat you down to tell you everything you thought is wrong. Know that everything you think will happen probably won't. Also, as long as you turn a profit, it doesn't matter.

Case in point, CBGB is the home of American Punk rock. It started in NYC in 1973 at 315 Bowery. It was started by Hilly Kristal, and those initials stood for "Country Blue Grass Blues." The home of punk began as a bluegrass music bar. Hilly knew enough to not mess with a good thing when The Ramones and Blondie took to his shit-hole music venue as their new home. The lesson is never look a gift horse in the mouth. The origins of that phrase are a person, given the gift of a horse, then looked at the horse's teeth to ungratefully determine how old the horse was. If you got something good going, run with it.

Andolini's has been the home to *Pokémon Go* clubs, Veterans' groups, and a group of swing dancers who dominated my late-night business. They would move the furniture to dance and have a great time. If they bought slices or not, I didn't care. People equal sales. Every group, club, or fad that has called Andolini's home, we have welcomed them with open arms. Each time we did, every club had the same story: "We love this place; (blank bar or restaurant) kicked us out. They didn't want us messing with their brand or current customers." Fuck that; you got money, if you're having a good time, you're accepting of others, then *mi casa es su casa*. Young, old, any race, any sexual orientation; I want you in my store. Business isn't about your preconceived bullshit; it's about entertaining people, all people, and making money in that pursuit.

FOCUS ON BASICS AT THE START

For getting your finances right, you must have a clean slate to start from. Before you open your restaurant, you should have a robust business model that's tested, reviewed, and evaluated thoroughly. Build out what's called a pro forma that states, "Here is how many people we expect to sit daily. At what level or rate we assume each person is going to spend based upon buying X item and X drink with an X side item. We expect to be X busy at lunch, and X busy at two o'clock, at three o'clock, at four o'clock, at six o'clock, and so forth."

After this, you need to nail down your expected daily, weekly, and monthly expenses to produce what you "plan" your profitability to be. This will be incredibly wrong, but you need a starting point to work from, and the pro forma is your best bet.

There's a *lot* you need to worry about during a new opening and a lot you don't need to overthink as well. Many new owners come to me concerned about having multiple styles of pizza day one. Even though they have yet to produce *one* style that doesn't suck, much less one that's amazing, some are concerned that their social media photos aren't getting enough likes – when no one is in their store. I've heard concerns such as adjacent businesses using up their parking spots—as if that's the reason people aren't coming in. These are all problems akin to rearranging deck chairs on the Titanic.

You've got to get your mind right (see what I did there, that's the name of the chapter, and here it is at the beginning of a paragraph which is also a reference to the movie *Cool Hand Luke*). When a problem comes into your worldview, you must ask, "Is this a problem I need to resolve today to make a profit? Not, "Can I fix this problem?" But, "Is solving this problem the absolute best use of my limited time?" That is the endless struggle of being an entrepreneur, and from my first-hand experience, I can tell you that question never goes away.

Food, service, and ambience: That's all you can take on at once. Each has a thousand subcategories, but those are what you need to move the needle. If it's not the wisest use of your time, delegate it out or put a pin in it for later. There is no doubt you will work hard; the uncertainty is whether or not you will work *smart*. Stop and take stock, evaluate the validity of each problem, and access your resources before executing. This is essential to getting through a store's initial push.

If you've been in this for a while and are still struggling with your business trajectory, you need to assess your weaknesses. Assess them and outsource them to people you can trust, that are affordable, that fit in line with your values. If you value speed and diligence, then find someone who is quick. If you value creativity above all else, then that person is not likely to be that quick. Whichever creative type you choose, decide and then use this person's skills to roll with your vision.

As time goes on, you need to assess not only your personal failing points but also the restaurant's failing points. You have to be able to suck it up and say,

"OK. We're going to change." The ability to pivot leads to success because if you aren't willing to change anything, then you're just on a path to death. Unless you are making insane level cash and you're like, "Don't rock the boat," you have to be able to move on a dime.

REMEMBER YOU'RE THE BOSS

Another thing to be keenly aware of when you're running your pizzeria is that, "*I own this mofo.*" You are the HBIC the second you say, "I am a leader." No one cares about your appearance. They care about your presence. Not your hair, not the bags under your eyes, your tan, or lack thereof; your staff, vendors, and customers need your presence. If you're a 6'5" super-built dude with a domineering appearance, it won't matter. If you walk into a room meekly with *zero* confidence, *you will get owned.*

I'll tell you this, some of the hardest, toughest, meanest dudes I ever met in the Marine Corps were under 5'4." That goes the same for women. Don't walk in thinking, "It's going to be impossible, and I hope someone listens to me." If you act like someone's friend, they will treat you like their friend. If you act like your employee's needy parent, they will treat you like their needy, nagging guardian. You know the one, the parent of a kid whose room is never clean until the parent begs them to clean it or worse than that, cleans it for them.

REMAIN ENTHUSIASTIC

Keep and maintain Day 1 Mentality. D1M means I don't know everything, but I'm dedicated to learning it and growing, and I'm excited as fuck to have you on this mission with me. D1M is feeling and knowing *I do* deserve this. *I will* do this, *and* people will want to work with and for me because I care about this more than any other boss they've ever worked for. I'll make my staff say, "I'm proud of what I'm doing with my life *because* I work here and for this individual whom I respect." It means looking at the world fresh, assuming you don't know it all but confident you can figure it out. The world needs followers; you need followers, but that can't be your role. You are not a follower; you are the leader.

Classically, people would say the world still needs ditch diggers, but now the world needs cubical drones. People who don't want to lead, people who don't want to make a decision. That's OK; you need these people, too, but you can't be that. You are in charge, and you need to proudly state it via not only your voice, diction, and mannerisms but your daily actions.

To the people who say, "You're not going to be able to do this," this isn't so much about showing them they were wrong. It's about you doing it against them for you, and for your future. Telling them they were wrong or proving it to them is a fun little cherry on top, but it is not the base of what you need to be fighting for. You need to fight for you. You need to know this is for you, for you and your family's future.

PREPARE TO BE LET DOWN

People will fail you. Accept that now. You are going to be disappointed. In the most blatant way, I want you to know this. *People will disappoint you.* Friendly employees will steal from you. People you trust will not show up. Family and friends you expected to eat at your pizzeria multiple times a week are going to come in once a year, if that. You will be disappointed if you believe or trust too much in what others will or won't do. Let that go and know that other people down the line will be reliable, will be loyal, will be your standard-bearers. Don't let the disappointment rock your world. Accept it as the inevitable turbulence of this flight.

STAY ON YOUR TOES

I've had several times where we had to pivot on very short notice. When we opened our second store, I realized that our logo didn't match our brand anymore. Our original logo was kitschy fun with a waiter drinking a beer and serving a pizza. This logo worked very well in a suburban atmosphere. As we opened our second location, built out with beautiful brick, dark wood, and a full bar, I realized we built it "too nice." Our brand had transitioned from goofy to an earnest culinary knowledge of pizza. I needed a logo that matched that. As you can see from the image, this is how we modified.

That's a change that sucked to deal with, but it was necessary, and I'm not alone in changing brands. Every lasting company changes their logo at some point.

LEFT: Original logo, 2005. This is not vector art, and that's why it's pixelated and crappy. Always build logos in vector. Vector is photoshop-speak for, "art you can blow up to the size of a building if needed". RIGHT: Reformatted original logo, 2007.

TOP: New branding word logo, 2012.
LEFT: New branding Andolini's symbol, 2012.
RIGHT: New branding Andolini's full crest, 2012.

Some logos have slight nuance; some have massive over-hauls. Apple's first logo was a large ornate dedication to Sir Isaac Newton. The current Apple logo has changed from a rainbow to a gradient view to now a solid apple. You're going to modify over time. You need logos that match your brand and evolve with it. Everything will evolve. The menu style, restaurant appearance, and even server uniforms will need to change. As it should. Change is growth. Growth is profit.

Whatever your brand is currently, if that's what you're locked in on, then everything needs to fall in line with it. If you're not sure, consider every aspect of your restaurant and ask the question, "Does this enhance the brand and user experience?" If the answer isn't yes or you don't know if it relates, then it's a no because it's not resonating with you or the customer.

If you can change your game up and admit when things are going wrong, then you can also overcome it. We've called an audible and changed up the central idea multiple times. Things we thought would be a massive hit just weren't. Sometimes, things that were dopey, throw-away, chance ideas became a customer highlight. When that happens, we enhance it and put it at the forefront.

This work will be a constant challenge. But it's your challenge, and *you can do this* if you choose to. It's on you to fulfill that promise to yourself with open eyes and confidence.

FOR THIS AUDITORY PALATE CLEANSER

No rock band personifies "Rock Band" more than Van Halen with David Lee Roth. The David Lee Roth years had a slew of hits, this not being one of them. This song's speed and bravado fall right in line with being confident about what your restaurant brings to the table. And the breakdown into Doo-Wop out of nowhere at the 2:50 second mark is especially outstanding.

Please enjoy,

"I'm The One"
by Van Halen

CHAPTER 3

THE IMPRESSIVE EXPERIENCE

You have eaten at great restaurants; you have eaten at bad restaurants. More likely than not, you have eaten at a ton of decent, just OK restaurants. Pizza places can get by on the "dive" atmosphere from time to time, but if you wanted to go back, then it wasn't shitty at all. If you thought about going back more than a few times, then it was better than OK. A pizzeria that has a place residing in your brain located in the food section, subcategory pizza, that triggers a positive reaction when your mind pulls up that file, is an impressive business.

You must be an impressive business to survive tomorrow. You can be an OK business and survive today, but that's not enough. We live in a state of constant distraction. Calls, texts, emails, social media, and that's just our phones. Family, work, TV, finances, if you want to stick out in someone's brain, you need to be worth the mental real estate. You need to stand out; you need to be impressive. If you do not make an impact as impressive, then you are not memorable and you'll never get a return visit. You'll just exist slowly on your way to death. In other words, store closing.

To be impressive means you uniquely hit their brain in a memorable way. You must trigger a happy synapse that initiates a positive response, a response they want their brain to feel again. An unimpressive business is *any* business that doesn't elicit that reaction.

The long hard truth I know to be a 100% absolute, indisputable fact after doing this for over fifteen years is that if...

YOU ARE EITHER IMPRESSIVE OR UNIMPRESSIVE; THERE IS NO MIDDLE GROUND.

I'll repeat, this time not textually yelling it; you are either impressive, or by default you are unimpressive. If you're unimpressive, then you and your business are forgettable; clichéd, dispensable, and on your path to the graveyard.

I am telling you the answer to the question now. Before I tell you how to be impressive, you must accept the doctrine of impressive vs. unimpressive to be fact.

For any real change to occur, one must first be aware, then willing, and finally prepared. Be aware now that if you aren't the best, *you don't matter*. Then be willing to change everything that isn't the best, however you define that. And last, be prepared via the minutiae and the daily grind of learning, growing, and training you and your staff, to be better every new day.

Most owners I meet fall into one of two categories; either they're humble, or they're arrogant. Not arrogant like an '80s movie villain but arrogant as in pompous about their restaurant's viability, and not very self-aware. It sounds like this: "We can't afford our labor, and we might have to close soon, but our customers love us, the restaurant is great, and it's the best pizza in the state."

Let's put that to bed right now. Your pizza is good but not great, and not everyone loves your restaurant. Yes, some people like your place, and some people play Bingo on Tuesdays at the YMCA; those stats do not make for a successful restaurant. You have some fans. But if you know them all, then it's not enough fans, and your Mom doesn't count. If you aren't killing it on all fronts, if something feels off, then read on. If you believe you are the best you will ever be already, then put this book down. Your ego has closed the doors to your brain. I can provide you no service.

If you set out to read a book on bettering yourself, then odds are you aren't a delusional egotistical asshat. Don't fall in love with yourself. *Ever.*

Here's a perfect example of an unimpressive business: The server comes by promptly, gives you a chance to read the menu, they then fill up the waters as needed.

They take the order like normal, music is fine, air temp is fine. The bill showed up on time, the food is fine. *So what's wrong here?* Nothing about this was special; these basic tenants are the price of entry, not the home run they came to see. These are things that *should happen*.

Nothing about that experience incentivizes a return visit. You need and live off of return visits. The only pizzerias and restaurants that don't thrive on regulars are in places in tourist traps. Places like Times Square where they churn out one-time visit tourists.

If there are four options in a tourist spot and you're number two, I'm not going to yours. No one wants the Second-Best Pizzeria in Town. People will eat at the most convenient restaurant in town, and that is not you. Gas stations are more convenient than your restaurant, and they serve pizza, too. Gas station pizza has become fine enough pizza that's faster and closer to the average customer than you are. Don't battle basic convenient pizza, the margins are too small, and the field is too large. Take the luxury approach to the business. Are you the most luxurious option, the most opulent, and every other fanciful word you've never heard used to describe a pizza restaurant? That means being impressive.

WHAT IS IMPRESSIVE?

The front of house (FOH) servers are interested in the customer and are being quirky themselves. The ones that care about what they're doing, that's impressive. They are having a fun time along with the customer and not at the expense of the customer. The food is not another basic ass pizza but has a story to tell. It hits the brain visually, as well as with taste. The menu is inviting with interesting names and a backstory on the baking process. This promise gets delivered in tandem by the servers. The ambiance of the restaurant is different, without clichés or inauthenticity. It's not pandering to be what the other guy is doing or what society says you must make a pizza restaurant look like. There's no generic photos of Venice on the wall and a "mob hits" CD on repeat. No endless repeat of four Sinatra songs you could recite backward. That's all bullshit. That's not you. *Be you. This isn't advice; it's a directive. Be you.*

If you really do listen to Sinatra all the time, then play the old Blue Eyes songs you love, not the song "My Way" forty times a day. If you like Rush, Boston, and Journey, play that. Be you and make it your own. I can detail all these dumb clichés because, at twenty-two, I did them all. I did them, assuming that following the well-worn path would lead me to success. It did not; it led to well-worn mediocrity.

Think about the last time you went to a restaurant. You went in, you sat down, you had dinner, everything was fine. Maybe there were a few things you could nit-pick, but there was nothing horrible about the restaurant. You got back in the car with the people you went to dinner with, and you said, "Eh, that was OK." Then someone else asked you a week or two later, "Hey, you want to go back to that restaurant?" and you said, "No, I've already been there." "Well, do you want to go back there?" "No, it's OK, let's go somewhere else."

Going somewhere else is just as bad as hating everything about that restaurant.

It's just as bad as hating it like it was the worst restaurant in the history of time. As if the owner cursed everyone out and threw your plates at the wall after taking a dump in the middle of the floor. In fact, in that worst restaurant in the history of time *experience*, I am way more enticed to go check that shit out. The dumpster fire of a restaurant scenario at least gives me a story to tell people about for the rest of the time. That's better than a mediocre no story basic-ass restaurant.

Everyone's seen what can be done.
We want to experience what hasn't.
That's where you come in.

FIGHT THE UNIMPRESSIVE

Now I could have come to this grandiose, climatic, massive takeaway in chapter 9; I'm not doing that. I'm doing it early because this is the most necessary item for your success. Do this now. If you run a restaurant, especially in the cutthroat pizzeria industry, you have to always be impressive.

Did you notice all the people you walked by today with their hair combed? No, why would you? That would be weird because that's just what people do. If someone has their hair up in a mohawk with the sides shaved off, you would take notice. Does that mean it's impressive? Yes, because it generated a reaction out of your brain to stop and take note. People noticing the positive aspects of your restaurant is how you stay relevant. Doing what's expected is just that, expected. You must do this, but that doesn't mean you're done. It only means you fulfilled the minimum requirement. Servers must fill water glasses as expected; if you can only get that right, you fail.

We're pre-disposed to believe that fitting in is the right thing to do. Middle school beat this into all of our heads. In the restaurant game, it is not the case. No one cares about you, no one cares about your business, no one cares that you put your heart and soul into it or that your house is on the line. No one gives one royally blue and white striped fuck about your problems. They only care about their potential enjoyment of their disposable income.

They care about having an experience. Did you give them a meal they could not have made themselves? Did you provide them with an experience that made their day brighter? Did they forget about the money it cost because it brought their family closer together? Did it make their date that much more memorable or made the middle of their nothing day with their crappy job not suck? Were they stoked to look good in front of their guest because they chose your pizzeria? Do they love this place because everyone had a great time and now they're the hero? This doesn't happen with the Venice posters on the wall and "mob hits" on repeat.

I had my first store for six years before we moved on to have a second location. In the second location, we got to build it from the ground up. *We built it*, with our effort, our ingenuity, and our sweat equity. We used brick from Kansas City road that was torn up and removed with actual tar and yellow street lines still on the brick. We made the floors from reclaimed barn wood before that was a thing. We built the bar ourselves; we took what should have been a $2 million build, but because we built it ourselves, we did it for $500,000. Everything still looks really cool, different, and interesting. By building it ourselves, it doesn't look streamlined; it looks unpolished and rough in the right ways. We haven't had to do a re-model because that look is timeless, and as a result, it's impressive. The ambiance was and is impressive.

When we built it that way, we didn't cognitively know that we were doing something unique. We didn't realize that by pouring our hearts out, it would show in the final result. After a few weeks of being open, I saw something I had never seen before. I saw a girl dressed up in a nice cocktail dress with a guy in a button-down shirt and tie coming into the restaurant. They walked right in front of me as I threw dough in the air performing dough tricks. These were not kids going to prom, not somebody that was lost. I realized that they weren't stopping in on the way to something else; this was their destination. It blew my mind coming from a suburban environment where all we had were families. We had done something different; we had created a restaurant scene, a place to be. It did happen as a happy accident, but the path to getting there wasn't. It was very purposeful. Upon that realization, we decided this would be the look we would use in any upcoming restaurants. When you finally hit it, you keep running with it.

As for our first store, we opened in a suburb six years earlier. It's not like it sucked. Well, it did at first, but we got better. Being impressive was always the plan, even if we hadn't put it to words yet. I'm sure that's your plan as well, but defining it makes it easier to attain. Coming from a suburban store in a strip mall, we never relegated ourselves to acting as if we were in a suburban store in a strip mall. We always acted like we were in the heart of Chelsea, Manhattan, where my family grew up.

CHECK EVERY BOX

Think and act upon what you can change *right now* to create an impact with the customer on the simplest of levels. Everything in the customer experience that could improve from when they walk in the door. What does the door handle look like, are the windows clean, to when they sit down? Is the chair some run-of-the-mill office supply chair, or does it have a cool feel and vibe to it that matches your brand? The servers' uniforms, do they even have one? Is the logo something that initiates a response and matches the brand you are looking to push out there? Is that person smiling, is that person engaging?

Does every aspect of this experience have something to catch the eye? Everything including the check presenter. Is it another run of the mill corporate free check presenter, or did you do something cool and different with it that resonated? Clipboard perhaps or maybe the bill folded in the shape of a kite. Is your logo on the check presenter, which is free, mind you, if you have your credit card company do it? These are opportunities to create an impressive atmosphere that resonates. This leads to return visits. The chances of them coming back after everything was perfect the first time is about 40%. That's life. If you kill it twice in a row, you bump up to 50%. If you do it thrice, you get what you need to survive and thrive. Three perfect visits equal a 70% return rate as your pizzeria becomes a part of their life routine.

That's an absolute scientific fact of the restaurant industry. You have to kill it three times to become a part of a routine; otherwise, you're a place they went to one time a few years back. So, stop and think about what you can change. Not just your food, not only your servers, what can you change right now that would affect the customer. Think small first. Think stupid simple things you could buy on Etsy or make yourself and then do that. Let me let you in on another little secret.

You can do whatever the fuck you want to do. It's America; we won the Wars—which wars, you ask? All of them, we fucking won them all. "But Mike, what about…" Nope, we won them all. You own your own business in America, so act like it. If you're reading this *not* in America, act like you are.

Consider this an invitation from me to you to act the part.

If you're not doing that, then you are doing a disservice to all the beaten slogs out there still working for the man. The people that dream of the day they can own their own business and do whatever the fuck they want. If you're doing whatever cliché you think you should do, then that's why you're fucking up. Go and have fun, go and be you, and put your personality and the things you like out on front street. Again, this is an invitation from me to you to *be you*.

Side note: Being you does not mean being a sleaze or a jerk and boozing at your bar and hitting on the host or hostess. It means playing the songs you like, serving the food you dig, and treating people the way you've always wanted to be treated.

When we first opened, we thought we needed more than pizza to entice the customer. We wanted to have something else to tie it all together. In our early years, we thought we should have a bunch of different kinds of ravioli. That seemed like a good idea; it seemed like the right thing to do, so we bought every frozen ravioli we could get. We purchased from a few different companies that were interesting and unique. It went on to do very well for us.

They became popular, and customers asked for them without seeing the menu. Then another Italian restaurant opened nearby and served the same eclectic, interesting ravioli. I then realized that that's not my ravioli at all. That's the frozen ravioli company's ravioli, and I sell it like this other schnook who sells it. The thing I bought is the same thing they bought. So, we're two different companies, buying McNuggets, but claiming neither one of us is McDonald's. It didn't matter what the name said, we were selling the same shit, so by default, we're not impressive anymore. They're not, and I'm not. This isn't imitation in the form of flattery; this is two bands playing the same cover song. I never wanted to do that. That's not what I got into this business to do.

That day I put the freezer on Craigslist, donated the ravioli to a homeless shelter, and we removed it from our menu. We said, "The next time we sell a ravioli, it'll be when we make it fresh." I'm proud to say the only ravioli we serve now is fresh ravioli made by us at our fine dining restaurant Prossimo.

FOR THIS AUDITORY PALATE CLEANSER

Faith No More never got their due credit for leading the pack of bass-driven Funk Rock right in line with the Chili Peppers. The overt sarcasm of this song that takes jabs at celebrity millionaires asking people to donate money was appreciated more after the band became more popular. I listened to this song, believing the band did care a lot about what they did, and I liked it because I always put a bunch of effort into things I took on. Sarcastic or not, I liken it to an anthem song about putting in work.

Please enjoy,

"We Care A Lot"
by Faith No More

CHAPTER 4

WHY SHOULD ANYONE BUY FROM YOU?

One of the lessons of traditional pizzeria marketing is that you must have a unique selling point or a *USP*. What is your USP? Constantly being pounded with a USP is the name of the game. I don't disagree that you need a unique selling point, but not merely one. You need unique selling points or USPs because "home of the spicy pie" is not enough to create a fiercely loyal or even regularly loyal fan base. Think about the brands you are fiercely loyal to, whether it's a clothing company or a tech company, something that you buy only that version of. The reason you are fiercely loyal is that it gives you a sense of pride and purpose in your brain when you purchase. It doesn't trigger the, "Oh, should I be buying this? Is this worth it?" Instead, it triggers the euphoric side of your brain.

Keeping the customer on the euphoric, prideful, and happy side of their brain is an art form. To accomplish this, the restaurant must be impressive at every point in the experience. Not only the food but the whole package, ambiance, and service included.

If you're getting by today on only one unique selling point, that's great. To that, I say this: you don't need a parachute to skydive. You don't; it is 100% absolute fact you *do not need* a parachute to jump out of a plane. The truth is, you *dooooooooo* need a parachute to skydive *twice*. You don't need to have multiple unique selling points to get by today. You must have a full customer experience steeped in unique selling points to survive tomorrow.

People will buy from you when you make them feel right about being at your restaurant. You will make them feel good when every aspect of the restaurant is unique and special. If they wanted basic, they would have stayed in their basic ass home. The easiest way to be special, unique, and impressive is with Easter eggs everywhere in your restaurant. These subtle nods ensure purchase pride and confidence while also relieving purchase anxiety. And when things do go wrong, you will take it as an opportunity, not a pitfall, to create another USP experience. That is why people will buy from you and why they will return to purchase from you for years to come.

CHOOSE INTERESTING MUSIC

So, what makes something a unique selling point? On a simple level, it means that the guy in your town that you're being compared to doesn't do it, but that's really not enough. A unique selling point must be in the elevator pitch fashion of, "Oh, I haven't been there. What do they do? Oh my God, they do this," and then whatever follows that. You want the elevator pitch to be something exceptional and easy to process. However, not everything is possible to condense into a pitch. If someone said, "What makes *Star Wars* so great"? It would be hard to put that into an elevator pitch. If you're a *Star Wars* fan, you would say, "Oh, it's just such an epic battle, with so many cool other things. I love (X, Y, Z) and (this and this and this)," and you would go on for a little bit. You could talk forever; it still wouldn't translate because *Star Wars* isn't conducive to explanation, it needs to be experienced.

But the great thing about a movie is it's not too dissimilar for what we do at a restaurant. Think of a soundtrack; in any great film, the music tells us what to think and how to feel. The score to a movie informs us to be fearful or happy for the protagonist. In your restaurant, your music sets your ambiance and gives the customer a feeling, but what feeling? That's for you to decide by being conscious that everything, even the music, very much matters. Every little decision matters.

When I first opened Andolini's, I thought, "OK, I'll put on adult contemporary songs." Nothing offensive, nothing too crazy, and that should do fine. Then I had customers say, "Oh, you know, I came to an Italian restaurant. I feel like I should hear Italian music." Before iPods existed, we would play a CD of Italian songs, and it got old really quick because that wasn't what I listened to. I don't drive to work listening to, "Hey Mambo."

If you listen to screamo death speed metal, no, I'm not suggesting you play that at your restaurant, but something that resonates with you is a wise choice. You're going to be listening to it a lot, so might as well have it be music you dig. I wanted to create a fun and approachable atmosphere. So, I chose fun, approachable songs. Originally on my adult contemporary list there was a bunch of Elton John songs, which you would think would be very appropriate. In actuality, Elton John's songs are depressing as shit. "Goodbye Yellow Brick Road" does not give the customer a feeling of happiness. It gives them a sense of longing and loss. If I want a fun atmosphere, "And I guess that's why they call it the blues," doesn't make me yearn for garlic knots.

The EJ classic "Saturday Night's Alright (For Fighting)" is upbeat. That's the feeling I want, and that's the type of song that works for my brand of Andolini's Pizzeria and me. You might be completely different. You might want synth-pop because you're going for a super cool vibe.

You might want to do the 1970s to early '80s punk or new wave, all viable choices as long as they match your brand. Again, you must build upon the brand promise to make a USP matter.

USE "EASTER EGGS" TO CREATE A USP

Easter eggs are an easy way to build extreme fan loyalty. Several movies have Easter eggs for keen-eyed fans to search for, to go to that next level of fandom. You want to make extreme fans by giving multiple levels of fandom to enjoy. Star Wars was incredibly more successful than Star Trek at creating fandom by having a slew more toys and merchandise than *Star Trek*. Being a part of people's mindset in more ways than one allows you to seep your brand into their daily lives. Allow your customers to go down the rabbit hole you create for them.

Here are some of my Easter eggs. At Andolini's, in the bathroom, I only play Billy Ocean songs on a loop. Three Billy Ocean songs. You read that right, *three* Billy Ocean songs: "Caribbean Queen," "Get Outta My Dreams and Into My Car," and "Suddenly." That's all that plays in the bathroom. That's an incredibly stupid Easter egg. But people talk about it. Why did I do that? Because one day, while I was enjoying my requisite sit-down experience, I realized that "Suddenly" is a delightful song to go number two to. When "Caribbean Queen" came on next, it struck me as a perfectly stupid idea. On a lark, I said, "We should make a whole separate amp play only Billy Ocean songs for the bathroom." And no one disagreed with me. It was the goof of an idea that everyone responded with, "Yes, we must do that." For about $300, I installed that amp and it became part of our Andolini's lore. It's so dumb, fun, and simple that it works. I've seen and heard customers ask each other about their Andolini's dedication, "If you're a real fan, you know about Billy Ocean, right?"

Another easy Easter egg is having a table that's set aside for a random individual. Make a sign that reads, "This Table Reserved For," put in some random celebrity name or the nickname of someone you went to high school with. Instantly you have people asking and wondering, "What's going on there?" You now are not cookie cutter. You are now not trying to be what everyone else is doing. You're doing you, and that's interesting. Do not attempt to do what has been done. It's been done and, therefore, it sucks and is lame. Even the examples I'm giving, don't be me, because you can't be me, because you can only be you, so do your own stupid fun Easter eggs.

You know who doesn't use Easter eggs? Lou Diamond Phillips (LDP). You get what you get with him and that's it.

YOU BE THE AMPLIFIED YOU AND HAVE STAFF BE THE AMPLIFIED THEM

Have fun out there, and let your staff be the amplified versions of themselves. Even if you have some speeches that your staff should give, they should be presented so it is interesting and defined by their personality. If you tell staff, "I need you to speak about these cocktails when you approach the table," and they just repeat your verbiage word for word, it will be bland. However, if that staff member is empowered to be goofy and fun and they go to the table and say something like, "All right, my name is Tom. I apologize that I'm not better looking, but hey, you're not paying for my looks. Now let's talk booze." It's a funny intro line that may apply to Tom if he's self-deprecating. If you see someone with that sensibility, you need to not only congratulate it but encourage it. These actions let your staff love where they work because they get to play up their personality. It also increases staff retention and improves customer loyalty.

NEVER COPY LOCALLY

If you're going to copy, emulate something that most people around you haven't seen. So, if you're in the middle of Iowa, sure, do something that you saw from New York that looked cool. But if you're on Second Avenue

NYC, no, you should not be trying to do what you saw the other guy do on Third Avenue. The best way I can explain it is as such: Don't be a cheap copy like *Acapulco HEAT*; be *Baywatch*.

MAKE YOUR FOOD A USP

One of Andolini's USP's is we make as many items as we can from absolute scratch. When we made that decision, we were closer to finding our voice. Great pizza was our thing day one but making everything from scratch was not. That stemmed from the time it takes to develop processes, and we didn't know any better. Once we honed in on that, and after we ditched the ravioli to make everything unique, we hit our stride. We incorporated freshly stretched mozzarella by pulling from curd daily, and it became a foundational USP. Then we made our own baguettes followed by casing our own sausage all in-house. We had made our meatballs since early on but tweaked the recipe and put it out at the forefront of our menu. We then sold the mozzarella as an appetizer, the same for the meatballs. By selling them on their own, it pushed that they got made on-site, which only increased sales and retention.

You must make things that are different. You must do something that hasn't been done. Do this in your own particular way, so you aren't selling a clichéd experience.

MAKE YOUR AMBIANCE A USP

Anything that only you do, your way, can be an ambiance Easter egg. For Andolini's, the addition of funny phrases or notes hidden on our pizza boxes, and all of our packaging is a fun nod to our customers who "get it." It's not a hard thing to accomplish and, no, not everyone sees it, but the people that do see it fan out and love it. On the checkboxes on the front of our pizza box, I have one checkbox listed "Secret Pizza." If someone asks, "Well, what's that pizza? I don't see it on the menu." The staff responds, "I can't tell you. It's a secret." That's a joke set up on par with a knock-knock joke. Don't underestimate the power of how simple it is to do compared to the impact it has. A joke on a box that the customer gets at that moment they inquire about it; it's fun. Dumb, yes, but also fun. Dumb fun that goes so far beyond stupid, it's clever.

I challenge you to look at everything that you're doing with your packaging. Look at your in-house items, everything beyond and including the food, and ask, "Has this been done before?" And, "How does this stand out?" I realized in 2011 that my parmesan and pepper shakers on the table were clichéd. I thought, "I've seen these same two brands of glass or plastic parmesan and pepper shakers at every restaurant supply store ever. Every pizza place has these same styles of shakers. I have to do something different."

Way before it became the fashionable thing to hand out at weddings, I found candle mason jars and fabricated my own metal lids. That way, it just didn't look like something else and became unique to us. I did not want the customer to see anything on the table they had seen before. At our second store, which would come to define our brand, we got delayed on opening by about four months. I was able to choose and develop every nuance of that store and cultivate our look. We made sure each chair was wood, but not the same wooden chair, and bought different eclectic chairs, so it had a unique vibe. We purchased several styles of chairs; however, we didn't consider how sturdy chairs should be. Lesson learned, buy eclectic sturdy chairs. When three people break through your chairs in a month, you learn this the hard way.

For our printed menu, I had the menu hand drawn in script and then copied that script rather than having it typed out. And I had the menu inside a tabbed file folder with space on the back for the customer to write their name. To make this custom meant getting with an office supply company to get logo-branded file folders. We chose that instead of going to a menu company and buying the old gold edge, black vinyl, insert menu holder. You know the one, the one you've seen at every unoriginal independent restaurant since you were a kid.

All these little touches set us apart and took us to the next level out the gate on day one for our second store.

Everything was about having something you hadn't seen before. That mindset will never change for us. People will never say, "You know what, I want to go to a new restaurant that does everything in the most basic way I've seen done a hundred times before." No one has ever said that, and no one will ever say that. People might say, "Oh, I love how they do this vintage style," but people will never say, "I love how stale and corporate you keep this place."

Even the name Andolini's has an Easter egg. The name comes from *The Godfather II*. Why *The Godfather II*? Well, for one, how dare you. And two, because Vito Andolini is Vito Corleone's real name. His name before he moved from Sicily to America. That name change never made a whole lot of sense to me because Corleone is a much harder name to say and spell than Andolini. I chose this because A is the first letter in the alphabet, and that mattered in 2004. This mattered because A is first in the phone book. Phone books very much mattered until 2008, so choosing a name easy to find in the phone book was very important. It doesn't matter now, but at the time it did.

Additionally, my Italian name is Carlucci. Joe Carlucci, whom I had seen on The Food Network, had a pizzeria already. I feared being sued for copyright issues, so that's why we did not name the restaurant Carlucci's. Interestingly enough, Joe is on the World Pizza Champions team with me today and is now my friend, so I guess you could call that a full circle.

INCREASE PURCHASE PRIDE AND DECREASE PURCHASE ANXIETY

To build a fan, you have to sell something special. The customer needs to feel happy when they buy it. You must reinforce their purchase pride when they buy it. And that feeling must be so strong that it alleviates any purchase anxiety they might have. A great example of reducing purchase anxiety is when people check in to a high-end hotel and the person checking them in says, "Oh, and I see you are in room 1108. I think you're going to like that room. It's a great room." You don't know if that person knows the view from the room or whatever reason why they think it's great. By saying that reassuring statement, they minimize your purchase anxiety and reaffirm that you were right to choose this hotel. They confirm your hope that you will have a great experience. The ambiguity one might feel going up in that elevator is now relief and purchase pride kicks in.

The same thing could be done at the table when someone orders a pizza. "Oh, that's an excellent choice, and one of my favorites." If the server says it to every single table for every order, no, it will not come off as genuine. However, servers with some stock phrases and a story about each menu item will make considerably more money for you and themselves. They build the level of purchase assuredness that increases the customer's guest experience. All the while minimizing purchase anxiety.

KNOW THE DIFFERENCE BETWEEN SERVICE AND HOSPITALITY

Here's the difference between service and hospitality. Service is someone knowing the fancy names of the sauces and serving your fork from the left. Service is pulling the plate from the right and all that kind of stuff that you'll get at five-star dining. That's high-end service. Hospitality is the down-home feel of a diner where they know your name and care about how your day is going.

In the hospitality industry, the goal is to make someone feel special and appreciated. In the service industry, the goal is to make the customer feel like they are purchasing something special, but not that they are special. I seek to give both service, albeit not pretentiously, and hospitality, without being hokey. Excellent service with approachable hospitality is the secret sauce to winning with blue-collar and white-collar audiences.

COMPETE IN THE SPITE OLYMPICS

Things will go wrong. When they do go wrong, it's good to have something simple to fix it fast when things are late, or maybe when an order was put in wrong. Ideally, a simple fix is an easy appetizer or dessert you can offer with minimal food cost. At Andolini's, our go-to is garlic knots or a free dessert. You won't know if a customer needs a fix-it order if someone doesn't check in on the table. This works better when it isn't only the server. Someone needs to check in with the table and build rapport, and then inquire how great everything was. If any signs show one aspect was less than, this person can now initiate a fix. If people aren't checking in with each table, such as a FOH manager, then you never get the opportunity to fix it on-site, day of, or potentially ever.

If something goes wrong and the customer emails you about it, that's a good thing. They are giving you one extra opportunity to fix it. Complaints are opportunities; *don't get annoyed by complaints.* It's important to do the following:

1. Hear them out, what happened to make the customer feel slighted. Regardless of whether it was misperception or truth, what led them to this place of frustration.
2. Offer a heartfelt response of understanding to their situation.
3. Map out a plan to fix this for them. Comp, replace, and/or double down on getting them fed or refunded.
4. Thank them for giving you the information. Inform them that their input will help you and

your company to progress and grow via an action plan you map out to them.

Hear them out, offer a response, solve the issue, and then thank them. Don't make excuses, don't BS the customer, and show you give a shit.

When things do go wrong, and I mean really bad, that's when you enter the next phase. It's not Restauranting 101. It's what I refer to as the Spite Olympics. The Spite Olympics is when kindness becomes a sport. When you're saying through actions, not words, "Listen here, mofo, you are going to take my free pizza, and I am going to make damn sure that you and I are right with each other. I will unfuck this thing I screwed up, that my business did wrong. I will do this because I will not have you going around town saying that we're shitty because we're not shitty. We've made a mistake, and I will unfuck that mistake right here and now." That's what I'm saying in my head. I am aggressively kind and using every ounce of spite kindness that my mother, who "suffered in silence," like she was verklempt listening to Streisand, taught me.

What's coming out of my mouth is that same message but with fewer F-bombs. So, if everything went wrong, I'll deal with it. I *will* make it right.

I also need my staff to make it right and have this same mentality. This outlook is more innate than trained to be a relentless people pleaser. So, this is how I evaluate that of a new manager.

Here's a question I'll say to an interviewee that's going for a management position. "Let's say we offered someone a free pizza, whether it was because we screwed up or they just got a free pizza. They come in, and with that free pizza certificate, everything went wrong. I can't offer them a refund. They already had a free pizza. And they just emailed or called to tell us once they got home, "Hey, I just want you to know everything was wrong. I have no intention of coming back to your restaurant."

What would you do or say?

I await their response and play it out from there.

The correct response is:

"Let me make this right. Please come back for a VIP experience on me. I will take care of you myself, and if it's not the best dining experience you've ever had in your life, please tell the world that. If it is, please tell the world that instead." That's throwing the gauntlet down that I can be great. We've screwed up. Please let me have the chance to show you this is not our standard.

I also say to the interviewee, "Imagine that we screwed up on a pizza. Now they're at home. Their kids need a meal, so they just popped open a microwave meal and fed their kids, and they call and tell you, 'Hey, I'm just telling you I didn't have your pizza. It was wrong. We have tried you a bunch of times, and each time you got the order wrong. My kid has dietary issues, and you get it wrong each time. I'm telling you, so you know why I'll never go back to your pizza place.'"

In that scenario, I see what the interviewee says. Typically, they'll say, "Oh, I'll deliver the pizza myself to their house as fast as possible. Even if they say they're already full, then I'll offer them another pizza again in the future as well as refunding their order." All these are the correct answers for someone that's advantageously looking to try and make it right.

This next-level Spite Olympics is one I've had to only do twice. The customer calls the restaurant, asks to speak to an owner. One person was positive their pizza had been messed with. They believed 100% that someone had put a hair in it, and the other person thought someone shook their pizza just to mess with them. This assumes the person making the pizza knew the end customer and sought to do this to a specific person. I realize you, the person reading this, doesn't know what staff I had when this occurred. Nor do you know who this person is that's complaining. In both examples, let me guarantee you this person knew none of my employees. Both times my staff was filled with a bunch of seventeen-year-olds, mostly overachiever kids, who wouldn't kill a fly, let alone mess with someone's pizza. That's how I knew it wasn't true. It's hard to convey this point to someone who's locked and loaded in assuming that everyone in the world is against them. It's challenging to convey this to someone certain that you messed with their pizza on purpose.

This is where the Spite Olympics takes a turn, and my guarantee to make this right gets put to the test.

I had one guy who said, "I am disgusted. I never even want to eat pizza again, let alone your pizza." At this point, I say, "Please tell me any food item that you would want from my restaurant or any restaurant in the Tulsa Metro area, and I will buy you dinner from them tonight. Not only that, but I will also personally deliver it to you." I've done that move two times ever. Only once did the person take me up on it and asked me to mail them a gift card instead. So, I procured their desired gift card, one fifty-dollar gift card to The Cheesecake Factory. The other person I offered this to was so impressed with my offer he re-evaluated his anger and opinion. He knew I was genuine and then started to doubt how possible it was that we messed with him on purpose. He came in, shook my hand, met my staff, and ended up apologizing to my staff, which I didn't need, nor did they.

For the one who took me up on it, No problem. Bought The Cheesecake Factory gift card and mailed it. Even in that scenario, I still won the Spite Olympics. The point of the Spite Olympics is not to buy The Cheesecake Factory gift cards. It's to overdo it so far to show what your brand will do to make the situation right, that you will go to the ends of the Earth. Not that the ends of the Earth exist because the Earth is not flat. *#Earthisround, #ThisbookisnotintendedforflatEarthers.*

That is what it takes to show you will do anything and everything to make things right. And that you do genuinely care about the customer. This type of solution only works if, guess what? You sincerely do give a shit about the customer. Caring leads to better reviews, better customer experiences, and leadership by example for your team.

FOR THIS AUDITORY PALATE CLEANSER

Lindsay Buckingham's breakup song to Stevie Nicks, played out in real-time as the band recorded their iconic eleventh studio album *Rumours*. Employees will come and go; the goal is to have your time with them be as focused and beneficial as possible. Ideally, I'd want everyone to work for us forever; they won't. I interpreted this song as go do what you need to do that's best for you, and hopefully, that is working with us.

Please enjoy,

"Go Your Own Way"
Fleetwood Mac

CHAPTER 5

WHY SHOULD ANYONE WORK FOR YOU?

THE NUTS AND BOLTS OF SMALL-UNIT LEADERSHIP

My first restaurant job was at Vic Stewart's, a high-end California steakhouse in the East Bay of San Francisco. In the late 90s, early 2000s, this was the San Francisco hotness; anyone who had money lived in the East Bay. And anyone who wanted to show off that money ate at Vic Stewart's. This was before the East Bay was inundated with high-end restaurants. I served *all* the East Bay greats. MC Hammer, Joe Montana, E-40, indeed a murderer's row of Bay Area legends.

At Vic Stewart's, I was an expediter (Expo), which means I ran the board of tickets and told servers which tables to go to. A job I didn't realize I would take to so fervently. Expo is harder at a steakhouse because entrees look identical but have separate doneness. They must get organized in seat order, and all you have to go off of is the "rarest" steak is to the right. A 20-Top (Top = seats at a dining table) of different temperature ribeye entrees, all different starches, organized by seat order, accomplished in less than 120 seconds, isn't easy. At Vic's, you couldn't be wrong because delivering high-end service was the name of the game, mess that up, and you're gone, fired, bye. Fifty applications are waiting to replace you.

At that restaurant I saw the dynamics of restaurant leadership. I had two direct supervisors: Tyler and Ron. Tyler was the Executive Chef and, by all fair accounts, a dick. He was the kind of jerk who would call your sister ugly to your face. Tyler was also a fantastic leader. There was another person who would run the shifts on Sunday, and his name was Ron. Ron was a great guy. Ron liked *Star Wars*, Ron liked jam bands and all the other random cool stuff that if you're eighteen, you want to know more about. Ron was cool.

Here's the thing about cool, cool doesn't mean shit when it comes to restauranting. On most nights, Tuesday through Saturday, when Tyler was running the shift, it was high energy. He was slapping his tongs and announcing to the kitchen, "Where we at, where we at?" He spoke quickly, with a lot of guttural distinction in his voice, checking in with each ticket. Sure, he might razz a server and curse like a sailor, but he kept things upbeat. I would show up at five, and before I knew it, it would be time to leave with tip money in hand and a solid feeling of accomplishment.

Then there's Sunday and Monday, the slower days that Tyler didn't work and his sous chef was in charge. This was Ron's time. Theoretically, this should have been even more enjoyable. It was atrocious. It was incredibly hard to get through those shifts, and I didn't realize why in my stupid eighteen-year-old brain. I now know exactly why. Ron was not a leader. Ron was a manager, or a shift babysitter, and a bad one at that. Ron was a talented culinary chef, but that didn't matter because Ron would complain. He would complain about how many re-fires there had been that day, he would complain about servers, and he would call out what time it was. "It's only 6:45? Jesus, will this night ever end?"

In my dumb eighteen-year-old brain, I'm thinking, "Yeah, this is going slow. These customers are lame tonight. Man, Ron, you're the coolest. Too bad everyone else sucks, and this sucks, and life sucks, and this job sucks, and we have another three hours until we even get a hope of leaving." Ron did not focus on morale. He focused only on the negative thoughts in his brain and externally processed it all shift long. *He didn't think about what people needed to hear; he just said what he wanted to say.* As a result, morale dipped, sales were shit, and nothing was right in the restaurant world of Vic Stewart's on Sunday and Monday.

The point is, you need not be a cheerleader on the sidelines or be super peppy. You must lead, and leading means having a plan and dedicating yourself to a vision. Leading means keeping exuberance, enthusiasm, and passion at a very high level. The beauty of this is anyone can do it. People will say, "Well, that guy's not a leader." Anyone can be a leader if they decide to do it. To those who want to never be in charge, don't want the responsibility, don't want the onus, then they should stay in the cubical. But again, that's not you, and that's not why you're reading this book.

I always wanted responsibility. I started Andolini's at the very young age of twenty-two. I learned what not to do many more times than I could wish, but I learned from every dumb error and took to heart what worked and documented it. When I was starting my second store, things got hard; I had to rely on my managers more and more. Some of my managers, especially the young ones, weren't trained for it. I had not invested time to prepare them and assumed they would take to leading as I had.

In this chapter, I'll first share leadership planning I received in the Marines and adapted for my restaurant. And I'll go in-depth on each way to use that planning in all aspects of the job; most importantly, mindset planning. This training got me out of that hole with store two and got my staff on the same page with me.

What follows is directly from my Andolini's Management Training Program. This is the theory portion of training, and *it works*. These are the fundamentals of being a leader that will allow you and your staff to stay in control. It will guide you to earn respect while maintaining the loyalty of your crew.

For all things leading, any system, any effort, any directive starts with this one mandate taken from the Basic Leadership Plan (BLP) direct from the USMC: *You are only as effective as your results.* Not your effort. Effort is *worthless* if it doesn't lead to results and a BLP ensures results.

Food cost, labor, morale, cleanliness, food quality are all your responsibilities and priorities. It can be daunting, or you can choose to own it. The way you get effective results is simple in nature.

FOUR-POINT BASIC LEADERSHIP PLAN

1. **Assess Your Resources and Surroundings**
   Example: I have a catering order tonight. How many staff members do I have for this shift? What do I need to accomplish this catering order to have it ready on time? Is it the right amount of staff for the shift, or am I understaffed? Do I have enough product? Is morale where it should be for the task at hand?

2. **Develop a Plan**
   Example: We need pizza delivered to a hospital twenty minutes away at 5 p.m. If I work

backward, and food needs to be on-premise at
4:50 p.m., what time do we need to leave the
building? When do we bag up pizzas, send round
one of the pizzas in the oven, and start to make
the pizzas? What's the time for each one of these
items as shown on the game plan?

ANDOLINI'S
EST. PIZZERIA 2005   GAME PLAN

Ordered By:		Ship Date:				
Name:			LEAVE AT:	DUE AT:	DRIVER:	VEHICLE:
Address:		Delivery 1:				
Phone:		Delivery 2 (if applicable):				

QTY #	What items do we need on hand for order?	Items Ready?

Start Time	What items need to be done at this time?	Item Done

Checklist	Item	No	Yes	If yes, how many?	Size

Individual order game plan

MACRO GAME PLAN	DATE:	ONSITE LEAD:	LEAD PHONE:
CUST: edwards party	CUST:	CUST:	CUST:
WHERE: Spain Ranch	WHERE:	WHERE:	WHERE:
IN OVEN: 4pm	IN OVEN:	IN OVEN:	IN OVEN:
LEAVE AT: 4:30pm	LEAVE AT:	LEAVE AT:	LEAVE AT:
ON SITE: 5pm	ON SITE:	ON SITE:	ON SITE:
DINE TIME: 5:20pm	DINE TIME:	DINE TIME:	DINE TIME:
PAY STATUS: CC paid	PAY STATUS:	PAY STATUS:	PAY STATUS:
PIZZA QTY: 10	PIZZA QTY:	PIZZA QTY:	PIZZA QTY:
PIZZA CUT: 12 CUT	PIZZA CUT:	PIZZA CUT:	PIZZA CUT:
SALAD QTY: 5	SALAD QTY:	SALAD QTY:	SALAD QTY:
PASTA QTY: 4	PASTA QTY:	PASTA QTY:	PASTA QTY:
OTHER ITEMS: Charc	OTHER ITEMS:	OTHER ITEMS:	OTHER ITEMS:
KITCHEN 1: Tom	KITCHEN 1:	KITCHEN 1:	KITCHEN 1:
KITCHEN 2: Joe	KITCHEN 2:	KITCHEN 2:	KITCHEN 2:
KITCHEN 3: Frank	KITCHEN 3:	KITCHEN 3	KITCHEN 3:
KITCHEN 4: N/A	KITCHEN 4:	KITCHEN 4	KITCHEN 4:
KITCHEN 5: N/A	KITCHEN 5:	KITCHEN 5:	KITCHEN 5:
DRIVER: Frank	DRIVER:	DRIVER:	DRIVER:
VEHICLE: BIG RED	VEHICLE:	VEHICLE:	VEHICLE:
ROAD TIME: 4:30-4:45	ROAD TIME:	ROAD TIME:	ROAD TIME:

All day game plan

3. **Communicate Effectively**
   Example: I have told every person *what* they need to do and *when* to do it in order to get this order out on time. I didn't just ask if they understood, I had them reply back to me their role in the plan and what they would be doing, and when. And I asked for any feedback on why this plan might not work. Our delivery driver gave feedback that the car I planned on using to deliver the order is low on gas.

4. **Execute and Follow Through on the Plan**
   Example: Due to the primary vehicle not having gas, we went back to step one and re-assessed our surroundings, found another vehicle that will work, inserted that into the plan, and communicated the plan. Then we delivered on time. Afterward, we re-assessed our vehicle fuel-up protocol to see where that failure point occurred and created a totally new four-step plan to ensure that it does not happen in the future.

How Does This Apply to Everyday Leadership?

This training will explore how these factors influence success by identifying our specific processes. I have broken those down into two groups, our Andolini's Priorities and our Andolini's Leadership Principles. Our

Priorities are the four aspects of our business. These are what my managers, my brother, and I focus on above all else. Our Principles are our leadership bylaws, which we look to again and again as our North Star.

ANDOLINI'S RESTAURANT PRIORITIES

With all your tasks and miscellaneous activities, it's easy to take your eyes off the ball. No matter what needs to be cleaned, what report you need to file, what evaluations must be done, etc., your restaurant priorities must always come first. Putting your personal checklist over these priorities is wrong and will lead to failure. For example:

1. **Service (The Customer)**
   The customer is *gold*. Service to the customer is king above all. No matter what the service issue is—not enough servers on shift, waiting too long at the counter, drinks not being filled— managers are expected to get out of the office and get the customer what they need, now! All duties are secondary to the customer being attended to with a *high* standard of customer service. Not merely an acceptable standard (which is unimpressive, as we've covered) but a *high* standard. If a manager is back of house (BOH) focused, they must be prepared to jump

in on phones or run food during a rush. If your managers focus on routine tasks during rush times, they are doing it wrong; 11 to 1 p.m. and 5 to 8 p.m. are not office times.

2. **Food Quality**
   If the sauce is burnt and the pasta is overcooked, it doesn't matter if the schedule for next week is posted or not. Never sacrifice food quality and attention to detail to get your tasks done.

3. **Ambiance**
   Be aware of the room. Is the music on? Is the air conditioning temperature right and functional? Are more chairs needed? Is anything dusty? Store leadership must ensure the ambiance is suitable first before they delegate daily duties like rolling silverware or folding boxes. Leaders must look for items *not on the daily checklists.*

4. **Staff Morale (or, What Brings the Food, Service and Ambiance Together)**
   Picking up cream at the store and taking two hours to do so, won't matter if the whole kitchen runs sluggish because of managerial indiscretions. The primary responsibility of managers is to ensure the staff is enthusiastic about the shift and getting things done. Staff

must understand why things are done the way they are, and ultimately, what will happen if things are left undone. Leaders should never leave their team for extended periods during the day unless someone else is the manager on duty (MOD)—especially during peak times or in situations with exacerbating circumstances.

If you nail food, service, ambience, and staff morale, the next part will be easy.

SUCCESS METRICS

- Labor: Less Than 30%
- Food Cost: Less Than 30%
- *and* 3% Minimum Growth over Last Year's Sales

AKA 30, 30, and 3.

The results of success are easy to see. When food, service and ambiance are on point, along with a staff that cares, then the fiscal objectives will get accomplished. Let's break each one down:

- **Labor: Less Than 30%**
  Keep an eye on morale and its ability to deliver excellence with the minimum amount of workforce possible. This is a fully baked number.

What I mean by that, is this is not just hourly employees or just base salaries, the goal of 30% or less assumes all payroll taxes and fees factored in. This metric is based on what leaves your bank to pay employees vs. what your bank says you deposited, not just what your point-of-sale computer says. This means everyone who gets paid is a part of this. If you operate as the manager and the owner, then your costs are part of this goal of 30% or less payroll. If you are running much less payroll than this, great, that's good, but make sure you aren't doing it at the cost of something else (like service or food quality). If you are over 30%, it's a safe bet your systems aren't tight enough, or your staff is too comfortable, and the job is too easy. Cross-training and a sense of urgency can reduce payroll quickly.

- **Food Cost: Less Than 30%**
  Focus on perfect, consistent execution of the product. Great food, moving quickly without over-ordering keeps this achievable. This cost should include all disposables of any sort. In this scenario, everything going in and out of your store in a week is part of food cost. If food cost is much below this, then again great, but is it at the expense of quality? If you are much

higher, you have waste, theft, and/or a poorly priced menu.

- **Three Percent Minimum Growth over Last Year's Sales**
  If FSA (Food Service Ambiance) on point gets you most of the way there, then assuming the average national Gross Domestic Product (GDP) growth, you should grow with it as well. If not, your store is dying and needs a revitalization, requiring a new basic four-point leadership plan. Start with what you think is wrong (i.e., staff, food, menu, marketing), and then go through the four points to attempt a course correction.

A seemingly great store with fantastic reviews and a line out the door is not a success if it does not make money. One more time: *A seemingly great store with fantastic reviews and a line out the door is not a success if it does not make money.* A successful store must hit these definable fiscal goals. High sales numbers don't matter without proper controls. If food cost is below 30%, and labor is below 30% along with year over year growth, that allows you 40% to pay for everything else. With those numbers, you should be able to walk away with a profit. Your staff is responsible for food and labor cost. You control the contracts with vendors to get the utilities, rent, marketing, and insurance prices all in line. If you walk away with a 1% profit, you are a success—every 1% more counts as an incremental gain towards wealth. If you break even, then get righteously annoyed and fix it. If you lose money, get mad and fight back.

ANDOLINI'S SIX LEADERSHIP PRINCIPLES

Leadership principles exist to create laws within any given organization. These principles work for any leadership situation but especially in a restaurant scenario. The Andolini's Six Leadership Principles help our leaders navigate any challenge.

The Andolini's Six Leadership Principles are:

1. Impressive OR by Default, Unimpressive
2. Ambiguity is Our Enemy
3. Lead with the Facts, Not Emotion
4. Perception is Reality
5. Be Proactive, Not Reactive
6. Lead by Example

1. Impressive *or* by Default, Unimpressive

We covered this already, but it deserves to be reiterated; if you just run through the motions you are dead in the water. Any member of staff who is just doing their job and nothing else must be corrected. If a staff member is complacent, a simple talk about their goals can be all that it takes to turn them around. Sometimes people just need someone to hear them out. Let them know that they are either impressive or unimpressive; there is no middle ground.

If you are not impressive, then you are by default unimpressive. On time, shoes tied, shirt clean, these are fundamental expectations; they don't manifest a customer's return visit. Massive smile, connection with people, going above and beyond, *seeking to impress* is the only way to get there.

Here are three examples of a server at a table performing a standard server sequence:

- **Example A: The Perfectly Fine Experience**
    1. The server takes their order.
    2. Food arrives at fifteen to twenty minutes.
    3. The food is perfectly fine.
    4. Server refills glasses one to two times.

This was an unimpressive experience that will yield no return visits for, on average, eight to twelve months. No positive word of mouth will be created from this visit, and if asked about your pizzeria, they will say, "It's OK."

- **Example B: The Server Sucked Experience**
    1. The server forgets their order.
    2. Food arrives at twenty-five minutes.
    3. The food is perfectly fine.

4. Server refills glasses one to two times.
5. No apology or interaction to gauge discontent.

This was a very unimpressive experience that will yield no return visits for, on average, twenty-four months. No positive word of mouth will be created from this visit, and if asked about your pizzeria, they will say, "They sucked."

- **Example C: The Impressive Experience Even with a Slow Kitchen**
    1. The server delivers an experience building rapport and putting their personality at the forefront.
    2. Plans ahead with pre-bussing and outward enthusiasm.
    3. Food arrives at thirty-five minutes, very late.
    4. The server apologizes at the fifteen-minute mark and prepares by setting up a free dessert order.
    5. Food is perfectly fine, but the server talks it up to make it feel special and more than fine.
    6. The customer appreciates the explanation of why food was late and happily surprised by free dessert.
    7. The server refills glasses one to two times and upsells their favorite alcohol.

8. The server knows the name of the customer, and they know the server's name upon exiting the restaurant.

A and B were both unimpressive experiences. Even though one was worse than the other, they *both yielded the same result: no positive word of mouth and no immediate return visit.* C shows the impressive experience from service alone, fixing a slow kitchen and creating a wow factor, *can yield a return visit.* This return will typically occur within forty-five days. Two more impressive experiences like this and the customer will make this restaurant a part of their dining routine and will continue to do so for the foreseeable future.

2. Ambiguity Is Our Enemy

If a staff member doesn't know where they stand with their manager, for whatever reason, it makes the staff member anxious, uneasy, and apathetic about their job. The manager might have no opinion on the staff member or potentially thinks they're doing great, and that's why they don't "bug" them. This can lead to the staff member feeling unappreciated, not seen, and therefore feeling like their role doesn't matter, and they lack purpose. This lack of communication results from lazy leadership and assumptive management that everything is "OK."

Ambiguity is like a bacterium growing in a petri dish, starting small and spreading. By getting in front of all issues and being assertive, staff knows where they stand and what the goal is. Clear, direct, and consistent communication leads to clear expectations and exact execution, even in the most chaotic of situations. Ambiguity can easily multiply in several aspects of a restaurant. Here are ways to keep clarity and avoid ambiguous forms of miscommunication:

- **Perform Staff Evaluations Regularly**
  Do these every three months at a minimum. Ask what their perspective is on what is working and what could be better. Ask what they think they could do better and support them in their growth. See where the job fits into their life goals and how they could be more fulfilled at work by giving more to the company. That way, they have a growth plan detailing what they will learn to get a raise and earn more responsibility. Also, these talks lead to clearly understanding an impending exit, for whatever reason. This avoids getting caught off guard by someone's decision to leave the company.

- **Log Notes and Shift Notes**
  These tools help alleviate ambiguity by communicating between staff members daily.

A log note is a summary of the day's events for managers to look at as a management team. "Johnny was late today by seven minutes, had a talk about punctuality, and gave a verbal warning." These can be logged in most online schedulers nowadays, as well as via several HR platforms. Whatever platform you choose, success will be determined by how consistently it is used and how convenient it is to apply to your daily grind.

A shift note is a list of things to make staff aware of before a shift, whether you address the servers or the kitchen or both. No matter what, before every shift, the team must be addressed by management. "Today we have an eighty-person catering order going out at 1 p.m. Thank you to Lisa and Tim, who came in on time today; they were the only ones to do so (point out the behaviors you want publicly.) We're 86'd (86 = out of an item) on eggplant because we rejected what was delivered today from the produce company. Any questions before we hit the open sign?"

- **Talk to People about Problems Directly**
  Take it head-on and come up with a resolution plan. Never let rumors or issues fester. Managers shouldn't pick every battle or jump on every issue, but they should be aware of rising problems to have a plan to deal with them proactively.

- **Communication Portals**
  Between group texts, emails, app notifications, and good old-fashioned face-to-face interactions, a manager deals with a lot of communication portals. Responding quickly and thoughtfully, but not at the expense of customer interaction, is how other managers and staff know what's going on. It's also how you stay aware of your restaurant's pulse. Not doing so leads to ambiguity, where the manager is not in control of the narrative—thus leaving themselves open to negative interpretations of their silence.

- **Build a Fence for the Employees**
  One of the critical steps of a manager's transition or the introduction of any new leader will be to set the tone for everything to follow. One way to do this is to "Circle the Troops" into a shift note that gives them all a sense of what expectations will be. This kills any ambiguity and decides right out of the gate how you will be perceived.
  In an introductory speech, you should:
  - Say your name and get their names if applicable.
  - Not overuse I, me, or my, but rather focus on we, us, and all of us.
  - Say you are open to addressing their concerns about the past and the way things are being

done. If you can resolve a stinging issue for
the staff fast, you have already won. They'll
be on board with your message and trust you.

- Settle their minds by reassuring them you
  are here to make their lives better, simpler,
  and more successful.
- Set the standard you want to be there for
  them, but that you will not tolerate XYZ,
  like tardiness, apathy, rudeness, etc....Build
  the fence for them to run in.

People thrive on structure and discipline. As much
as it may seem annoying to them at times, the opposite realms of chaos and ambiguity are much scarier and
harder to work in. Your worth is in your ability to provide stability and growth. *To be a leader is to enable those
being led to thrive.*

3. Lead with Facts, Not Emotion

Facts are inarguable, and they get the point across
quickly and directly. Emotions are rooted in opinion
and hearsay, often causing debate and division. It is critical to keep a disagreement rooted in facts to ensure the
points are agreed to and a part of a solid resolution plan.

- **Socratic Method**
  One effective way to help people grow through

effective communication is to use the Socratic method to help someone discover the solution on their own. The Socratic method is a form of a cooperative argumentative dialogue between individuals, based on asking and answering questions to stimulate critical thinking. It draws out ideas and underlying presumptions without the employee being told what to do. Instead, the employee answers the questions to arrive at a sufficient resolution themselves.

Example:

Manager: "You were late twice this week; what do you think I should I do about it?"

Employee: "Write me up?"

Manager: "OK, let's say I write you up, what do you plan to do differently?"

Employee: "Set a second alarm so I make sure I wake up on time."

Manager: "Do you foresee this being a problem again, if you do that?"

Employee: "No, that will fix it."

Manager: "What should happen if you're late again?"

Employee: "You suspend me or let me go?"

Manager: "OK, I accept your plan, sounds good."

In that very basic example, the manager leads the employee to decide their own path and plan, the direction is their idea, so it is inherently agreed upon. If an employee tries to deviate or say something like the following, you can then course correct to more questions.

Employee: "I don't know, maybe you could let me get away with it this one time."

Manager: "Assuming I let you get away with it and not everyone else for the same offense, would that be fair? What problems could that cause in the restaurant?"

This way, they follow your logic, so it becomes their logic.

4. Perception Is Reality

Perception is nine-tenths of reality. No matter what a leader tries to communicate, how hard they work behind the scenes, and all the work done that no one knows about, what the team believes to be real therefore becomes real. Even if it is not the truth, people will believe it is, and their response to a situation will be based on what reality is to them.

To combat this, leaders must manage their image to their team. Leaders may not always be liked, but they must be respected. Having both traits would always be ideal. If a leader continually works all night setting the team up for success but drags ass the next day without explanation, the staff will eventually think their leader is tired and lazy. Explaining what you are doing behind the scenes and overexposing hard work is a strong way to control a narrative. It might seem counterintuitive to work hard for the show, but if a leader doesn't show their work, they leave themselves susceptible. Once a bad perception starts, it doesn't change by only stopping the bad behavior; it changes when it's overcorrected publicly.

Example:

Employees' perception: Staff thinks a manager believes they are above manual labor or "doing grunt work."

Manager response: Words matter less than actions. The manager can't say they aren't above grunt work; they need to show it. The manager will have to jump on and run the dish station for multiple shifts. They will need to get on their hands and knees cleaning below equipment in front of every staff member for weeks to kill that perception.

If a manager says, "I don't care what a bunch of teenagers think about me, I know how hard I work." That's a dumb public declaration rooted in apathy about a negative perception of management. This lackluster perception will therefore continue to fester and thrive in ambiguity. Negativity will continue to control the narrative while the manager lazily does nothing about it, and proves the negative perception to be, in fact, true.

5. Be Proactive, Not Reactive

No one wants things to go wrong. However, does your planning *intend* to put safeguards in place ensuring things do *not* go wrong? Planning takes effort, not a simple assumption that one can rely on unspoken norms to see a task through. To be proactive, you must assume Murphy's Law that if it can go wrong, it will go wrong. If you leave the schedule open-ended as to who will pick up an unwanted shift, you will find no one taking that shift and be down on labor when you need it most. If your system has a safeguard against shifts going unfulfilled and a redundancy plan for what to do when that inevitably happens, then you have *proactively* implemented a solution to this problem.

- **Inspection vs. Expectation**
  In school, there was always that teacher who gave you pop quizzes every week. It was known that they were anything but pop quizzes; they were frequent spot checks. Everyone knew they would get one. As a result, students continually studied to prepare for the inevitable pop quiz. In other classes, it was easy to put in a little effort last minute and just cram the night before the final exam. In contrast, the pop quiz teacher *always* had consistent expectations for daily effort.

Students put in effort throughout the semester and *were better for it*. The pop quiz teachers were more respected because everyone knew you couldn't pull a fast one on them.

To be proactive in leading a team, you must give pop-up assessments. It must be understood that tasks and duties will get checked and that some work will be considered unacceptable. No restaurant has a 100% success rate with 0% inspection. If any pizza can get sent from the kitchen without a final inspection to ensure it's perfect or else, then why would the last person who sends the pizza to the customer ever care to check? The answer is some would out of personal pride or avoiding a vocal complaint, but most won't, and "good enough" food will be what's commonly served. If any amount of side work effort was acceptable, then why would anyone put forth any more effort than the bare minimum to get through the day?

People will always take the path of least resistance. If that means they can do whatever and not get called out, then eventually doing whatever will be the standard. If putting out a bad product will be noticed, and more work will be done as double duty to correct it, then clear expectations to do it right the first time will become the standard. In time, the path of least resistance (avoiding double duty and do-overs) melds into efficiency and exacting execution.

- **KISS: Keep It Simple, Stupid**
  Any good system and organization doesn't take a manual to understand. Don't create a Dewey decimal system of filing away HR files. Alphabetical works fine.

  Side note: This happened, I had a staff member who wanted to organize the staff files based on start date and job code instead of last name. I asked, "How will anyone not completely knowledgeable of every current staff member's standing ever be able to look someone up?" That person stared at me with a blank face. Keep it simple, because that is stupid-proof.

- **Streamline Everything**
  Ford designed the assembly line for the Model-T in 1908. Before then, creating a car was an extremely laborious endeavor and cost large amounts of money. With the Ford assembly line, they could do it fast because each person handled their role. When each cog in the system efficiently performed their role in an optimized process, the whole build moved more quickly. Shop workers weren't putting the tools down to move onto the next part. Employees stayed in the

zone and became more efficient at doing their singular task, faster. A leader's job is to focus and find ways to move smarter so the crew can move faster. No one wants to work harder to get the same or weaker results.

Examples:

- Bussing tables with a bus tub instead of three trips to the table using only what your hands can hold.
- A dishwasher moving efficiently to bring dry dishes to stations in bulk rather than after each wash load finishes.
- All interviews getting scheduled back to back, not scattered all over the week.
- Running your weekly errands all on the same day and same time, so it's one long trip instead of fifteen small ones.
- In the kitchen, prepping mass quantities instead of just what you need to get by for the day (pending freshness and food waste).

- **Shoelace Logic**
  Imagine a marathon runner at mile ten, and their shoe becomes untied. If they said, "I can't stop to tie my shoe, I'm running a marathon," then the next sixteen miles will not go well, all to avoid the fifteen seconds it takes to tie their laces. In a restaurant, not stopping to tie the laces of the

prep line, bar rail, or expo window because the staff is "*soooo buuuusssy*" is shortsighted and stupid.

No matter how busy you get, you can stop to tie your shoes. When tasks in front of you or your staff pile up to a seemingly insurmountable level, the right move is to stop and compose yourself. Put items back and keep the workspace clean, maintain order, and call for help when you need it. Doing it any other way means you're not streamlined. At any point, at any time, on any day, take fifteen seconds to refresh and re-assess. Don't just deal with what is right in front of you, but ask yourself, "What is the wisest move to do right now to get this done faster?"

- **Being Intentional to Guard against the Unintentional**
  Lots of mistakes are unintentional. Any mistake that *is* intentional would be a fireable offense because that would be a malicious act. However, having the foresight to *intend for a problem not to happen* as I shared earlier, is what sets a leader apart. They think about potential problems and how to fix them before they happen. They think out situations and prep out the whole scenario. Great leaders also communicate to make sure everyone is on the same page to avoid confusion.

It can be redundant, but redundancy produces flawless execution. The steps of the leadership plan dictate this as a must.

6. Lead by Example

The most important rule for any leader is to lead by example, but *what* example though? It's a multifaceted question that requires thought and diligence.

People hate hypocrisy. To build a strong team, staff members must care what leadership says and does. For any task given, the team needs to know that the person giving it would be willing to do it themselves — and that it would probably be done better by them, if so.

However, keep in mind the *Maestro Caveat*: Some people teach better than they perform. Some are a better Maestro to the orchestra than they are a violin player. It should be rare in an unskilled job like working in a restaurant, but sometimes the people you lead are better than you are at a task. This should be a rarity and not the situation for most tasks. A sixty-year-old football coach doesn't run faster than their running back. The coach understands the speed it will take to be a success and can train their team for it. At Andolini's, an example is a manager who knows when BOH employees should throw dough to entertain the crowd. They know this is the moment for dough throwing even if the manager isn't a great dough thrower; this is maestro leadership.

The trusted maestro leader should be the default person to answer questions and make daily decisions. A maestro decision is which prep task is most important as well as bigger situations like dealing with an unhappy customer. Another mandate of maestro leadership is that what is said matters, and when the maestro speaks, staff listens.

Solid leaders are dependable. Bad leaders don't do what they say. Solid leaders create solutions. Bad leaders create excuses. Solid leaders own their mistakes. Bad leaders blame others.

- **Care, Be Genuine, Have Passion**
  If you want what you say as the maestro to be heard, you need to care and speak passionately. Caring —no one can force someone to care, *but* you can lead others into caring by leading by example. It's easy to follow an infectious attitude of positivity. People who care about their job make it obvious in their actions. All action needs to come from a place of caring about everything. Caring about the customer, the staff, the food, and the ambiance should be at the front of any restaurant maestro manager's actions, always. When people don't care, they get apathetic. Both caring and apathy are deeply contagious.

  What do you want staff to unconsciously think?

"That person cares about our results and seems fun; I want to follow their lead and care as well."

or

"My boss barely leaves the comfort of the office to check in with us; I'll milk this job until something better comes along."

An apathetic person isn't necessarily a bad or mean person. The opposite is also true; passionate people can be pains in the ass. The truth is passionate people move the needle, increase morale, and produce sales. Apathetic people slow time to a crawl and bring the mood down. A cook who points out how slow a night is going, complains about returned food, and constantly whines will destroy a shift's morale.

A hustle spirit of, "We got this," and a push for more mindset gives people the feeling that what is being done matters. People want to be a part of things that matter.

Being "genuine-fake" is fake—most people can see through fake, and they hate it. Fake is lying, pretending, not really caring, not willing to work an issue out. The type of person who does nothing all day then walks into the kitchen to say how great everyone is doing. Then that manager goes back into the office to hit the vape pen and check their Facebook. People hate this manager.

It's obvious when someone is genuine. People who are genuine are dedicated to helping find solutions from small to large problems. To be genuine, you have to actually care and have true passion.

Enthusiasm is a lot like passion. Passion is the drive to want to be the best. A passionate individual who cares about others gains the trust of everyone around them by being genuine. This person is unstoppable when it comes to achieving the unwavering support of their team. This is how wars are won.

- **Exploit Pride, Not Labor**
  One way to succeed greatly is to inspire employees to push themselves to attain better results. At the same time, exploiting or exhausting people can create drones that grow resentful. Pride is our friend. Pride in what people can create or do can generate high morale in even the most difficult of situations. Healthy competition and a general, "We did it!" attitude can turn a soggy day into a productive one.

  Another solution for pushing staff to have self-pride: let them judge themselves. Let them review their own performance as a prelude to formal evaluations. Most workers will be tougher on themselves than their manager would. This allows managers to align themselves with those they lead. You can either agree with their honest self-evaluation or advise them to lighten up. This is another example of the Socratic method.

- **Work for the Company, Not Yourself**
  To lead by example, you must be an employee on the team with a seat on the bus. You're still the owner, but you are in it with your team. At Andolini's, the atmosphere is people work hard as a benefit to the team, which benefits the individual. Staff must be motivated to strive and take pride and ownership in the organization. Otherwise, they are looking for an easy out as a shortsighted goal for the day. *You don't have to be the owner to take ownership.*

  Another parable I heard once and I tell my staff: There were once two construction workers. One clocked out at 5 p.m., the other worked until all the steel they had was put up. The second worker did it because he liked seeing tasks accomplished. The first worker worked until his time was up and called it a day. The second worker ran projects and teams because he liked finishing tasks he was in charge of. As a result, more responsibility was given to him. This turned into more projects given to him, which turned into more profit for the company. He became invaluable to the company. He sought ways to do jobs quicker and easier since he had first-hand knowledge of what it took to do the job right. His insight proved invaluable. The first worker had to work until 5 p.m. til the day he died. The second worker never had to work at all anymore because he retired early.

To be in charge, you need to lead. Working for the team's goal, being the maestro, and caring about everyone along the way. This is the path of least resistance: enthusiasm for the work.

- **Leading by Example Means Leading with Motivation**
  Anything can be accomplished with proper motivation. For many, money is a key motivator. For others, fear of losing what they have worked for motivates them. In this work environment, identifying people's motivation, as well as your own, is important. Other than money, you'll find that acceptance, respect, and the desire to be pushed to learn or to grow can also be great motivators. Being self-motivated for any of these reasons can help you get more out of yourself,

which, in turn, will show others how to be self-motivated.

THE PITFALLS

Beyond the six leadership principles are some pitfalls to remember. These are facts of the industry that can and will take any good leader down:

1. Restaurants Die without Adrenaline

It's fascinating how slow a restaurant with two tables at 3 p.m. can be on ticket times. Sales are not proportional to staff. Not appreciating the dead hours can and will destroy a restaurant's reputation quickly. Some restaurants just avoid non-rush times by closing in the afternoons. Andolini's doesn't do that because it leads to fewer sales and a confused customer. The customer is left wondering, "Are they open now? I don't think they re-open 'til six, let's go somewhere we know for sure is open." So, we don't close mid-day, but that means we must be "on" all day.

It's vital to keep standards up at all times of the day, not just during the rush. The primary focus must always be the customer. No matter how busy or slow it is, staff must take care of customers first. Lazy management will allow prep tasks to supersede the customer if it means leaving sooner. This is a callous decision. And bored staff get sloppy and can forget simple protocols. By keeping people busy with cleaning when there are no customers, malaise can be avoided.

2. The Status Quo Will Always Drop Off without Leadership

If there is no pressure to improve, then what is acceptable will slowly degrade over time. Apathy will infect tasks, food quality, and attitude. Problem areas, wherever they may be, must be addressed constantly. Standards must be upheld, or inevitably the status quo of acceptable behaviors will erode.

3. The Broken Window Effect

It's easy to tell when you're in a not-so-safe neighborhood by how the environment is treated. If a window can be broken and no one cares, then who would care if weeds grow and trash is everywhere. The same applies to a kitchen and restaurant. If a light bulb can go unchanged, a sign can be disheveled or half hanging, then why not let everything go to shit. Frankly, it likely already has, from the customer's perspective. That is why every nuance, no matter how small, must be maintained to instill a sense of order in a restaurant.

Managers and true leaders are doers. They get shit done, even in a world full of don't-ers. The doers see the problem before the customer. They are the leaders who recognize the substandard before the entry-level employee. They must address it via the basic leadership plan to assess and remedy any problem.

4. Shortsighted Goals

People always choose the path of least resistance. *Always.* The problem lies in that sometimes people choose the wrong path because they don't evaluate all paths. Often, people assume the easiest path is the one directly in front of them. Before the cart was invented, people just moved items by hand. Stopping to think there is a better way, working to create the cart, then using it for large loads, was the *indirect* path of least resistance. In a restaurant and in life, the direct path of shortsighted goals is easy to see versus a search for the best path of least resistance—even if it's indirect. This is a reinforcement of the Ford Model-T assembly line concept.

5. Messing with Their Money!

The quickest way to lose all your goodwill from staff is to be dishonest or cavalier with pay rates, cash, tips, or checks. Andolini's uses a system where managers aren't in front of checks because we direct deposit all payments. Imagine, though, a FOH manager who takes a 20-top and then says they only trusted themselves with that big a table, and then took the full tip. Think of a kitchen manager who promised raises to everyone then goes back on the promise. What would that do to morale and staff retention?

SUMMARY

By providing stability and focused leadership, you allow others to become better people. It's not about being a power-hungry asshole; it's about being a focused leader. You can execute greatness when you avoid ambiguity and abide by these principles. These principles allow staff to feel safe, stable, and that they're operating in a dependable work environment. That is how staff is retained, and profit is made.

FOR THIS (NON-AUDITORY) PALATE CLEANSER

Here is my favorite story about an employee screwing up in the history of our company. It's important to appreciate good moments, but it's a lot easier to appreciate fantastically bad ones.

Please enjoy...

"The Story of Ad-Chay"

I'll change the name to benefit the subject of my story. Let's just call him Ad-Chay. Ad-Chay had a very unique day with me in September of 2009. We were delivering pizzas to a local kids' bounce house. It involved cutting and boxing eight sixteen-inch pizzas and delivering them to this kiddie funhouse.

On this day, we didn't have our regular pizza boxes. We had blank white pizza boxes because our logo boxes got delayed. I got a call from Ad-Chay while he was delivering, and he said in a very high-pitched but slow stoner-y voice, "Mike, I don't know how, but the pizzas I am delivering right now are upside down." I said, "How is it possible that the pizzas are upside down?" He said, "I don't know Mike because when I got the pizzas, they were upside down, and I put them right side up. But now I went to deliver them, and they're upside down."

I said, "Ad-Chay, that doesn't add up. I don't understand how they were upside down but not upside down, but now they are upside down when they shouldn't have ever been upside down because the pizza comes out of the oven and it goes right into a pizza box." He said, "Like, I don't know, Mike, but like, the pizzas I had were upside down when I got them. But now, I thought I had fixed it, but they're still upside down here."

There's only one thing I could do, which was go to the cameras. Upon looking at the cameras, I saw Ad-Chay. He sees the pizza boxes, he's about to load them into the bag. He looks left, he looks right, he looks anxious, hurried, and frantic, as if, how did this happen? And then takes a stack, a whole stack of eight pizzas, and in one simultaneous stacked deck swoosh, inverts them to be what he believed to be right side up.

What actually occurred was that, because the pizza boxes had no logo on them, his high-as-a-kite stoned-ass believed they were all upside down. He flipped them, thinking he was correcting this "problem" but actually *creating* the problem he was trying to avoid. Once he believed them to be right-side-up, he proceeded to then deliver them... except, of course, all of the pizza was now upside-down upon delivery to the customer.

That night, I remade the pizzas, looked at him in the eye, and said, "Never, ever show up stoned for work again. This is your one get-out-of-jail-free card. Do you understand?" In all honesty, it was totally worth him being high as shit and losing eight pizzas to save that video footage, which I still have.

Ad-Chay stopped smoking weed, became a manager for me, did great things in the Tulsa metro area, and now has a family. I've had plenty of Ad-Chays work for me. Not all of them have given me stories of that caliber, but they've all been good people. And I'm happy and thankful they've become even better people, hopefully *after* leaving my restaurant.

Oh, this one other time Ad-Chay texted the whole group thread of every manager who worked for me...and it was his pillow talk to his then-girlfriend consisting of, "Are you napping yet, my beautiful?"

We took screenshots and made them into t-shirts for all the employees, because that's what you do in that situation.

CHAPTER 6

COMMUNICATION TO STAFF

HOW TO BE HEARD AND
BUILD MORALE

When we started Andolini's, it felt natural to have a Christmas party. Sure, why not? We had a bunch of seventeen- to twenty-one-year-olds, and we made sure that the event was fun. We kept it goofy, and for many years it would be a simple fun party. Some snacks, order some Mexican food, give out some fake awards, and then do a relay race.

At first, the relay race was whatever absurd things I could come up with, for example, "Drink two-liter bottles of Sprite and run around the restaurant." Also, "Eat Cheetos and jump up and down, then put your shoes on your hands and call yourself Shoeverine." Again, genuinely dumb stuff but designed to get people out of their heads and build morale.

We kept doing this at different locations and with different morale-building outcomes. Finally, once we had five locations, I realized all the stores should compete against each other. As a result, in 2016, we had our first *AndoMania* event. Each store, competing in events you would see at the Las Vegas Pizza Expo. Events like Fastest Dough, Largest Dough, and Acrobatic Pizza Tossing. Then we got into bake-offs along with the fastest silverware roll. All this hoping to win the championship title belt. We did a take on the official WWE championship belt and added our logos to it.

All this cheesy stuff was and is a morale builder. People like to compete. People want to be able to say, "I'm the best." If you don't give your venues the chance to prove who is the best, to have that notoriety, then you're missing out on an immense morale opportunity.

Staff morale is incredibly essential to productivity in a restaurant. Building that morale is done primarily via verbal interactions. Physical actions as well but mostly verbal. What you say vs. what staff hears is rarely the same. This chapter will delve into communication techniques that result in increased morale. These techniques will keep staff productive, because they know they are in a stable environment. It is crucial to provide this base to allow staff to feel safe to work and grow in your business. It's only through staff retention that you will ever see gains in service and experience.

AndoMania has been a defining characteristic of the restaurant. It's unique to us, and it's something that we take a lot of pride in. At the end of every *AndoMania*, I keep it just like that first Christmas party and hold a relay race. We now call it the "Feats of Strength," a reference to Seinfeld's "Festivus" episode. Staff compete in eating massive amounts of cheese puffs, then they do crazy team drills. All this occurs in the middle of the night in a Tulsa parking lot, during the height of summer. *AndoMania* has become one of the mainstays

Alfredo Herrera, 2016 General Manager of Andolini's Tulsa location, victorious with the Andolini's Championship Belt at Andomania I. Alfredo went on to become our Area Director as a result of his morale building abilities.

that binds my team together. It's the morale glue that helps someone stay loyal. Loyalty in your brand makes employees dig your restaurant and view other restaurant jobs as less than.

True staff developments, not obligatory staff developments, but true staff developments are where loyalty and camaraderie are not only built but solidified. Building that kind of loyalty is the task of leaders who are heard when they speak. Constant effective communication is how you do it. The goal is always to increase morale, but what is morale?

WHAT IS MORALE?

Morale is the feeling of enthusiasm and loyalty that a person or group has about a task or job. Morale is critical to the environment at your restaurant because success and reputation are directly determined by the morale of your team. High morale isn't just so the days go by easier, it increases employee retention and staff throughput. High morale equals profit.

COMMUNICATION 101

One of the greatest factors in any leadership environment is communication. It is vital to always be aware of how communication affects morale in your organization and to always look for proactive ways to use communication to remove barriers that negatively affect the team.

Someone's voice has a lot to do with how they communicate and how they are perceived. Tone, speed, rhythm, volume, and the actual words chosen all make up how someone's voice sounds to others. Additionally, mannerisms, body language, and facial language; a lot goes into a conversation other than what is actually said.

Just because all people aren't currently aware of all this, doesn't mean that all these factors aren't changing the perception of what is being said. It's important to be consciously in control of your body, aware that the body is an instrument of communication. Body language determines how a person is perceived and interpreted.

Here is a quick breakdown of body language basics:

- **Intent**: To know what to do with your body, you need to know the intent of your message. Before you choose your words and the body language to go with it, you should know the goal of the conversation before starting it. Knowing the intended outcome will affect all decisions made during the conversation.

- **Conviction**: "I think, perhaps, maybe we should one day, possibly"—If it's worth saying, then say it. Say what's worth stating with conviction. Leave out all these additions to communication that will be perceived as weakness and dilute any message conveyed. Don't use "like" or "um." Don't be a marble mouth that can't put words into proper context. "Like" and "um" are the crutches of imprisoned speech. It's best to break free and let words speak without speed bumps that add nothing to the message. Believe and be proud of what you are saying. Otherwise, why even say it?

- **Diction and emphasis**: Words need to be processed into the subject's head in a palatable way. It's good to avoid speaking in a slow and monotonous way that will cause them to zone out. Highlight the words that are paramount to the message, so they sink in. One should never slur words, and people should always think of what they plan to say before they say it. It never hurts to practice what needs to be said, as well.

- **Hands and arms**: They should help improve body language. It's good practice to match the type of conversation. Speaking vividly with hand movements can show passion in a message. However, you wouldn't use wild hand movements while speaking condolences to an employee who had a death in their family. Hand gestures have a place, and it's in adding to animated, impassioned speech. Be aware of folding your arms as this conveys judgment; if you want to come off as judge-y, then fold away. If you want to appear open to what is being heard, keep your hands behind your back. I advise servers to do this when at a table with a customer. All these mannerisms give social cues that can help or hurt your intended goal.

- **Body placement**: If you stand on the side of someone vs. right in front of them, it will influence the mood of the conversation. Talking to someone at a bar is non-confrontational because you are next to them. If you speak directly in front of someone, it feels authoritative, like an interview. When the intent is to come off like a friend, say it next to them rather than in front of them. If you are scolding an employee, do it face to face.

- **Posture**: Don't slouch or lean, be upright, and keep your chin up. Keep eye contact, and don't speak to the ground. Do this, and your message will be interpreted as worthy of attention and authoritative.

Subconsciously, everyone makes decisions based upon all these factors. Your brain won't register them all, and the result of your mannerisms might not match your words. Being conscious of mannerisms takes time and practice. Having a checklist of things you want to work on is a smart way to check it and fix it. I wasn't looking people in the eye and said the word "basically" too often. I noted it and worked on it until it was out of my vernacular. These days, overuse of "like," "literally," and speaking in vocal fry is pervasive (google "Bachelor Vocal Fry" if you need an example). These are year 2020 vocal crutches, but it will change to something else; it always does. A good example of weak speech: "It like, literally killed me, the way he just basically sat there while we all worked." No, it didn't, because if it *did* kill you, you wouldn't be able to recount your nonsensical story.

Communication Drills for Staff

This is a simple fun drill to use with staff to teach vocal inflection to communicate better with customers and each other. It's one of my favorites because it demonstrates, without debate, how much more we communicate with inflection than we realize. Seeing staff come to this realization during the drill has always been fun for me. I very much enjoy immediately seeing growth and development from the team, and this drill does that.

Purpose: this activity is designed to help you understand how both verbal and nonverbal cues affect communication.

1. The goal is to say the word "Dude" in a different context. Each round, we focus on a different emphasis on what we are trying to communicate.

   So, say "Dude" so it conveys each point. (You can do this exercise on your own first, but with a group is best.)

   - Say "Dude" in a happy way. Keep it light. Say "Dude" in the way you would greet someone you haven't seen in a long time.
   - Now say "Dude" in a stern direct way that tells the person you are serious. Pretend they said an offensive word that won't be tolerated.
   - Now say "Dude" in a hopeful and encouraging way. Pretend you're congratulating someone who just completed a marathon.

   Think of five other talks or emotions you convey in conversation and get them across in a one-word "Dude." Come up with them as a group activity.

   Do ten versions with you and/or your crew until the giggles are out. Do this until everyone learns how to use tone as a tool outside of the actual words of the message. Likely, this will be the first time your staff has ever considered the value of what they're saying beyond their words.

2. Say this tongue twister, not unlike the dude exercise. Use this full sentence to control your

phrasing. Avoid stumbling over the words to curse inadvertently. Get your point across with a sentence that has nothing to do with your worded messaging.

"I am a pheasant plucker. I pluck mother pheasants. I am the most pleasant mother pheasant plucker, ever to pluck a mother pheasant."

Say it with this emphasis in your voice:

- Say it happy, as if you're having a great day and want everyone to know it.
- Say it sternly, as if this person has been late three times, and it's not sustainable.
- Say it hopefully, as if you know it has been a hard shift, but we're almost done, and everything is coming together.

If your tone and diction are both on point, the message resonates more thoroughly. This is a goofy exercise, but it creates change.

MANAGEMENT COMMUNICATION GUIDELINES

Now that you have the inflection down, here's a rundown of the basic management talks you will and should have with staff. These are the typical conversations that will be necessary for discipline. What follows are best practices for handling these kinds of talks.

Tell Them Why

"Because I said so," is a reason but not a good one. Explaining the importance of a task puts it into perspective. For example: If a server asks why they must roll so much silverware at the end of a night, don't say, "Because that's the rule." Explore the experience of what happens when tasks are left undone. Help them understand there is no way of knowing what the morning crew will have on their plate tomorrow. By rolling a lot of silverware in advance, we ensure success. It's especially important to expect the unexpected, such as an unexpected rush. That will inevitably happen. For all tasks you delegate, make sure these aspects of the task are addressed:

1. Define what is being asked of them.
2. Explain why it is important.
3. Let them know it is a team effort.
4. Create and use a timetable for completing the task. Follow up and check-in via inspection that they got it done properly and in that timetable.

Keep It Light

For first-time offenses and things that aren't deal-breakers, do this. Have a slightly jocular sensibility; this can make the medicine easier to swallow. In a non-confrontational manner, say something wasn't correct; it gets the point across easier. Laugh with the employee rather than at them, and they are more prone to hear you.

Avoid mocking the individual; instead, make fun of the incorrect action. Joking should only go so far, though. Never ridicule or chastise someone for doing the right thing. A non-functional work environment example is when everyone shows up late, and the one person who shows up on time is considered a kiss-ass. Anytime there is an environment where someone is mocked as a "kiss-ass" and it is acceptable, the whole team is destined for mediocrity at best.

Never insert a joke or prank into a duty list, schedule, or anything that needs to be dependable. That confuses employees and contradicts the work you've done to create reliable systems and boundaries. Joking in a restaurant is about having fun so people don't hate where they work. The goal is that no one takes themselves too seriously, but everyone takes the work extremely seriously.

When To Get Harsh

Being negative and disappointed can be used as a tool. Positive reinforcement works for most employees; however, some employees won't understand unless they're in trouble. These employees seek the lowest common denominator in life and need to have their priorities and habits adjusted. I never advise yelling, but sometimes explaining directly and sternly that something is unacceptable is the only way to break through.

Set the Tone

Setting the tone is essential. Setting the tone with enthusiasm and positivity is a best practice. The most important question to ask all day in every situation with every crew you lead is this:

Is this room better because I am in it?

Am I adding to the morale and intelligence of the room, and if not, what can be done to change that? Remember that your attitude is a choice, and it determines the crew's morale. If you clock watch or complain about customers, etc., it creates a downward spiral of negativity. Keeping morale high is the responsibility of the manager leading, even in the most trying of times. When bad things occur, a manager is tasked with keeping things light to maintain staff morale. Being self-motivated and positive encourages others to do so as well. Positivity is the straightest path to getting big things accomplished easier. With all that said, it's OK to be stern and fun. Don't be fun and a doormat.

Avoid These Topics

Setting the tone means not engaging and shutting down these conversations the second they arise. Shut this shit down immediately, don't wait to hear it out, *shut that shit down*. Topics like these cause people to get pissed or, worse, fired.

- Sex: salacious details are not for those you work with. Shut this talk down.
- Religion: one believes in that, and one doesn't. Again, don't engage in this. Nothing productive will occur. It's not your role to save souls or ruin them while on the clock.
- Gossip: what and who did what, and how, etc. It's not needed information and only causes unnecessary drama; avoid it. How much someone makes in salary is also gossip; never accept compensation gossip in your restaurant.
- Violence: any talk leading to a fight is one notch below the actual violence itself. Violence can never be tolerated. "Come at me, Brah," is not in a functioning team's vernacular.
- Politics: red or blue state, you're bound to anger someone; nothing good comes of it. Leave it alone.

Have Humility as a Boss and/or Manager

Looking overconfident and acting like a know-it-all will not earn you points. Employees getting talked down to gets old, especially when coming from someone who doesn't back up what they say. It reverts to everyone's dislike of hypocrisy. Always seek to under-promise and over-deliver to your staff as well as your customer.

Be confident but never cocky. You can always learn more, and your staff can be a part of that. You will, at one point, be wrong; an ability to admit that is how you save face and earn the respect of your employees. Someone who can't admit fault doesn't gain respect. They are sniffed out as phonies and mocked by their employees.

Create a Team Environment

We know to exploit pride, not labor. Do we know how to maintain that pride across all sections of the restaurant? It's human nature to unify against a common enemy. As a country, we're better than that country; as a state, we're better than that state, down to town, team, age, etc. This cannot be how your restaurant operates. Competition is excellent; civil war is peril. Here is the typical infighting that occurs in a restaurant. Know these, so you are aware of how to shut it down.

FOH vs BOH

- Both sections are equally important. Officially they are equal. It's the chicken and the egg. Great food gets customers; excellent service keeps customers and creates new customers. The customer is gold, so the front lines are incredibly important during the rush, but dedicated BOH makes it all possible.

- The skillsets are entirely different; to try and compare them is *foolish*. Serving is about comfort and kindness; a server sweating a mile a minute while gasping for air is not how you win return visits. While a BOH employee gasping for air is not ideal either, a BOH employee continually moving, keeping their head down to get tasks done is ideal.

- BOH kitchen employees are the lifeblood of the restaurant. They make what people came to purchase. It's on them to do it quickly and effectively, which takes skill. A well-trained BOH employee is not easy to come by, and the cost to replace a good one costs as much as a great server's ability to upsell.

- Servers must be aware they can make more than a BOH employee for using their brain more than their sweat equity. A server that helps out at dish and gives clear ticket instructions is appreciated. This behavior, along with being courteous to kitchen employees, keeps morale and motivation upbeat.

- BOH must understand the mental agility it takes to anticipate the needs of several tables. The server's job is not to get flustered while appearing charming and knowledgeable. Their job isn't to deliver food but rather to enhance the customer's experience. If service is being done right, it will appear more natural than it looks.

Day Crew vs. Night Crew

- For FOH, you have two completely separate customer groups. A quick service lower tipping group vs. nighttime crew's more extended tables with more significant demands. All are hard jobs, and all deserve respect. The morning crew must set the night up for success since they have more time on their hands. Night crew must ensure a great experience and close strong to set up for a fresh start the next day.

- The same rules apply to BOH. One is mostly prep and early hours; the other goes late into the night with crazy ticket lines and more cleaning tasks.

- Communication, understanding, standard-setting, and empathy for the other shift are crucial to peacekeeping. Have a total refusal to let your restaurant get divided. Always explain what the other shift doesn't see and kill any unrighteous complaining.

Cooks vs. Pizza Crew

- Both serve a separate purpose. Both require different skill sets. Do not tolerate conflict from your staff by having both sides cross-train, even when they are set in their roles.

Employee vs. Manager

- There is a time for GM's and managers to play bad cop. Management can't ever hold antipathy for the employee. Their job is to keep great people, maintain standards, and motivate staff. Managers must appease all-star staff members sometimes, and that pill can be hard to swallow. Managers need to make wise, egoless decisions.

- Some staff will just get mad when they don't get their way; that's fine as long as they still respect you. Never tolerate disrespect, and never give staff reason not to respect you. If you ever do, fix it by admitting fault and course correcting.

- Naive employees will view even-keeled managers as lazy and having an easy life. The reality is that all responsibility falls on management, especially the GM. It might sound weird, but a successful GM is the one not doing anything, only observing the customers. A GM in total control of their role has all systems functioning properly. The successful GM is there waiting in case something goes wrong. They're ready for the drunk customer, AC issue, an accident, and everything else that can fail. All these issues, when they fall to the GM's feet, they will resolve as the leader of that restaurant.

Our Restaurant vs. the Customer

- *They pay our bills; shut it down.* "But the customer doesn't get it, they..." They're not paid to get it; we are, so *shut it down*; if someone stupidly and naively has antipathy towards the customer, *shut that shit down.* For example, if the staff gets pissed that a customer came in five minutes before you close, your response should be, "Oh, can you believe that they came in, while we were open? What the shit were they thinking?!?" Say that as mockingly as you can, because it deserves mockage. The mentality of pushing away business is death in a restaurant. *Shut that shit down.*

Our Restaurant vs. Every Other Restaurant

- It's our job to be the best. It's not our job to say anything negative about others to prove we're the best; that we leave to our customers.

- Part of being great is not talking about it. Louis Vuitton ads don't bash Target handbags. Rolls Royce doesn't spout that their car is more beautiful than a Kia. Proper success culture is to be classy and speak about what excites you, not who you believe you are better than. To any pizzeria who says they're better than you, don't even address the argument. Speak on how many great things YOU do day-to-day while their name never gets mentioned. You will only come off petty shitting on your competition, not believable, but petty.

Have Conviction and Consistency

Don't wimp out—most employees respond well to straight-talking managers. Managers who give mushy or evasive answers such as, "Let's revisit that later," "We'll see," or "I'll try my hardest," will often bob and weave their way into oblivion. It's fine to say, "I don't know," as long there are some fact-gathering questions that show interest in formulating a serious answer. That's the kind of consistency that people appreciate.

It's important not to send contradictory signals or give different answers to the same question. That's a common rookie mistake. You don't want to hear things like, "You said something completely different yesterday," or, "I'm not sure if you've approved or denied my request." To avoid this, stay consistent.

Never Let them See you Sweat

With your tone and speech, project a calm demeanor even in the face of chaos. *Be a rock* in times of turmoil, and people will respect you. To do this, take a deep breath and step back. Figure out what the wisest decision is in that moment, make the call, and execute. To know the wisest decision, think out the end result of your actions. Like playing chess, consider the next three steps of what will happen because of your words and actions. Don't concern yourself with what you want to say, only with what needs to be heard to get your desired outcome.

Maintain Control

A sensible leader is aware of the power and authority they have but also when to use it. They don't overly threaten to use or abuse it. Controlled managers keep their cool and stay in control by standing up straight and projecting a sense of bearing. For example, a manager should never allow their speech to be cut off and should take control of an irrational employee like a petulant child rather than an equal. Managers and employees are not equals, and the leading manager shouldn't treat them as such. If an employee's words or actions have a manager seeing red, the leading manager must regain their control. Take a deep breath, self-evaluate, decide the wisest decision, and then speak. Avoid being baited, control the conversation from the start to where you want it to end.

Reward Excellence, but Don't Play Favorites

It's natural to like some people more than others. However, the rules and standards must be the same for all. At the same time, rewarding those who go above and beyond is capitalism, and it's a good thing. People who do their job right and contribute to the workplace deserve some level of special treatment. The best servers should get the best sections and not have to do anything that keeps them away from making money. Playing favorites based upon looks or social stature outside of work is where it becomes unacceptable favoritism.

Don't Let Passive Aggression Fester

One of the most common workplace problems is passive-aggressive behavior. Frustrated employees can become passive aggressive. They don't say what their problem is and aren't working to fix it. Instead, they walk around angry, hoping their anger will get people to notice their plight. Typically, the person they want to see them has no idea they have a problem. As a result, the passive-aggressive employee is letting something ruin their day hoping it will affect someone else's day. Watch out for those who swallow the poison pill and hope the other person dies. These people are false martyrs obsessed with destroying your crew's morale.

When problems surface, communication is the only answer. If you notice someone else with a problem, communicate with them. Anyone who is visibly frustrated should have the chance to cool off and move on or voice his or her frustration and work through it. Not doing either is unacceptable. So yes, being in a lousy mood and doing nothing proactive to fix it is unacceptable. This rule is twice as important for anyone in front of customers. If you ever hear a server say, "I'm pissed, but I'm fine in front of my tables," *never* let them anywhere near a customer. Work through and resolve their problem; if it's impossible, send them home and address it tomorrow.

Don't Assume Employees Are Mind Readers

What you say is not what people hear. What you believe you are is not what you're perceived as. It's never 100%

aligned. If you're a great communicator, they align most of the time but never all of the time. Odds are you could stand to be a better communicator. Not being heard and perceived as you want to be is very frustrating and typical of leaders in restaurants. As a callback to earlier, to know if someone understands what you've said, you need to insist they recite it back to you. If they can explain it to you, along with the reason it's being asked, then and only then will you know you were heard. When you don't do this and bloviate your thoughts to get it off your chest, you are pointlessly externally processing.

Externally processing is when you take all your thoughts, bottle them up, and release them on someone in hopes they tend to them. This is also called a brain dump where you say everything on your mind and assume everyone else not only listened to it but additionally heard it. I brain dump from time to time, but with it, I also take notes and insist on what I dumped is said back to me. I deal with the discrepancies of how I was interpreted, and then I collect my notes and revisit them later. This way, I gain some traction. Engaging in a brain dump without a plan is naive. To assume anyone will understand and follow through on a brain dump is foolish. This type of communication leads to frustration. The speaker will be happy at the moment to get those thoughts off their chest but frustrated when what they say isn't acted on correctly. The listener then becomes frustrated when the way they interpret the brain dump goes awry.

Imagine you say, "Clean the refrigerators and the office this weekend. You got it?" The employee answers yes because to say no would make them feel dumb when the question was, in fact, dumb or at least not specific. The employee wipes down the refrigerator inside and out and sweeps the office floor. By Monday, you are pissed because there is still flour in the coils of the refrigerator compressor. And the office has papers on the desk that aren't filed. The brain dump didn't work. A lack of specific and direct task delegation has led to this.

You might find out later why they misinterpreted your direction, or you might write them off as dumb, and they write you off as a taskmaster. They're embarrassed, and you're angry because of your lousy communication. You didn't verify or have them restate what exact tasks were to be done in a manner that bred discussion and clarity.

Your staff are not mind-readers. You are not a mind reader. This means communication takes patience, investment of time, and pause to verify. It's not easy to do. It's not hard either; it's just something that needs to be done if you want things done right the first time.

Bad communication is like an '80s situation comedy. When I watched *Three's Company*, it would be so frustrating to watch, even though that was the point of the humor. The situation was always a misunderstanding blown out of proportion. As a kid, I'd think, "Come on, Mr. Furley, just ask what the problem is, let Jack explain it, and avoid this whole mess." Instead, one person assumed one thing, Jack and Chrissy assumed another thing, and then Janet's out in the cold, because, well...she's Janet.

That's a situation comedy. In real life, stopping, asking, verifying, and caring about the other person's interpretation leads to tasks getting done the first time. Genuinely caring about their understanding of your stated goals is how you get your stated goals to be their interpretation.

FACILITATE OIL CHANGES

Around every three to four months, the oil in my car gets low enough I need to take it in and kill an hour waiting for the oil change to occur on my vehicle. It's not that big a deal. It just needs to be done, and then it's on to the next thing.

Some employees need an oil change in the sense that every three or four months they just freak out, something rises to the highest level, and they spin out. They might've said, "Oh, I got it. It's not a big deal. I can handle it." And then one day they can't handle it, and they just blow.

Random blow-ups can be frustrating when they happen multiple times. If you have a well-trained person that does a quarterly freak out, it's worth it to hear them out and come up with a plan to avoid this in the future. Develop them as a person and, in the kindest way possible, put up with their bullshit. Do this because they're solidly trained, and you don't want to lose solid people over a minuscule freak-out.

Chalk it up to the oil change, accept your wasted hour, and deal. Maintain a solid employee who knows what they're doing on your team. It's preferable to training someone else who might not work out.

If they violate a rule, a rule that's a deal-breaker, then no, don't keep them on your team. However, if they freak out or get super-stressed, even breakdown or cry, then that's just part of the game. It's your duty as a good person and leader to facilitate their growth from situations like this.

Stay Above the Fray

Managers who warn the staff what not to do, and then see staff do it anyway, are often tempted to give them a big, "I told you so." The manager may know they're right. It may seem like the right thing to let staff know they screwed up on this one. As a result, there is now an embarrassed, ashamed, ego-broken crew with an absence of trust. Confidence lies in the leader who keeps their cool and gives appropriate corrective action. Bad example: You catch an employee turning a trip to the trash into a smoke break. You scold harshly. "What did you think? I wouldn't catch you? Do you think we're dumb here? Go inside and consider yourself without a break for tomorrow." If you haven't set a precedent with this rule and consequence for all staff, you are just searching for fights. You could be right about whatever rule violation has occurred, but this employee is now inclined not to want to work for you. Now they'll be smarter about how they find a way around your discipline. There is an easier and more effective way.

Good example: Don't say a word while they do it; just look at them and let them know you see them. If you feel the need to engage, ask questions rather than dole out punishment. "Is this your smoke break (inquisitively)? Oh, it's not? Well, OK then. Do you know how many breaks you get per shift? You know why we have that rule, right? OK, cool, please don't do this again." This is a small discipline talk. If the problem persists, tell them what punishments will occur if the behavior continues. At all times, work *with* the employee to get past their bad behavior. If they do it openly to disrespect you, stay above the anger, and engage them in a talk about expectations and what the result of their actions will be. Stay above the fray; stay the adult. Never enter the sandbox with an employee and argue on their level.

CHAIN OF COMMAND MEETING COMMUNICATION TREE

The communication tree lets a message flow through leadership. From the owner to general manager, to kitchen manager, to the FOH lead, to server and back house employee. Everyone following the chain of command. This is my workflow of communication as an owner. I, as an owner, have an owner meeting between my brother and I, along with our area director to go over all things top level. Issues we see in that meeting are taken to the general manager meeting we also have once a week. At that general manager meeting, we go through whatever issues and items at the store level exist. We list them all out. Then we document who is going to be the Directly Responsible Individual (DRI) to take each item on. We either address the issue or add it to a to-do list to be executed by next week's meeting. Those managers then have their meetings with their own staff. They address whatever issues were brought up at the general manager meeting. The staff then should be talking with their individual employees daily before every shift.

This is the shift meeting we mentioned previously. A pre-shift, or shift note, meeting has to happen on every shift. This meeting must happen for both the FOH and the BOH. Even if you think you have nothing to say, there always is something to say. You can even say, "Everything worked out great last night. The cleaning list was fantastic," or "You guys did everything right." I suggest you point out everything right, so people don't only hear the negative and, in turn, seek positive praise. If you need to point out, "Hey, we can do better on this," or "We have a big order tonight due at eight o'clock," all these things should be done as a shift note. For FOH servers, a shift note goes over what things are out of stock along with specials to be upsold.

If a restaurant does not hold a pre-shift meeting, they are taking what they perceive to be the path of least resistance. It is actually the path of disenfranchisement and a lack of communication that builds antipathy. It's the path of the most resistance, as a simple two-minute meeting sets everyone else up for success and makes things easier. If someone's politicking or taking too long at meetings, yes, you can pull them aside and say, "Hey, these meetings aren't the time for that." Communication and effective delegation make your life easier.

I've heard before, "Well, everyone knows what to do. We don't need to go over it each week." This is a statement steeped in mediocrity. Assumption leadership does not work.

Staff must respect the chain of command and be a part of it. I'm OK with the staff directly asking me a question, but as a leader, I have to reinforce the communication tree and not bypass the chain of command. If their question should go to their supervisor, that is who I direct them to. If they have spoken to their superiors and gotten no response, I want staff to have the ability to go directly to me as a fallback. This check and balance is a part of the chain of command for the communication tree of a successful organization.

I have staff that worked for me in 2005 that still work for me in some way now. Kids who were servers in high school are now my IT consultants and catering liaisons. They've grown up and are in their thirties now, as am I. We essentially grew up together, and the bonds have only grown because I invested in them, and they have taken that investment and doubled down on it with our restaurant.

A lot of staff have led separate lives, but it is my hope and goal that when they leave, they are better for the journey of being an Andolini's employee. That we showed them what a healthy functioning business looks like. I hope they look as fondly on it today as I look at Vic Stewart's, my first significant restaurant job. I hope I'm not thought of as a jerk like Tyler, but if I saw Tyler today, I'd shake his hand and say, "I owe you *big time*," because he taught me how to restaurant (restaurant is a verb in our world).

FOR THIS AUDITORY PALATE CLEANSER

Metallica faced harsh criticism from the metal community after cutting their hair and releasing two sonic influenced albums; *Load* and *Reload*. They then double-downed on their affront to preconceived notions of what a metal band should be by releasing a symphony-backed, orchestral live album with the San Francisco Symphony Orchestra. Recorded live at the Berkeley Theater in 1999, this song was created solely for this album and never recorded in studio. The song details assuming peace and sanctuary are coming from the light at the end of the tunnel when, in actuality, it's a train barreling down the path to take you out.

The freight train you don't see coming occurs in a restaurant when you assume something is taken care of and set forever. That's the moment it falls apart. By never loving what's been accomplished but instead continually asking what else can be done, you stay ahead of the pitfalls. Metallica reinvested in themselves to do something new, to create something no one asked for but never knew they wanted. It's an unyielding drive that led to the Symphony & Metallica album, *S&M*.

Please enjoy,

"No Leaf Clover"
by Metallica

.

CHAPTER 7

DO I SUCK?

AND WHY "YES" IS A
GREAT ANSWER

t's 2007, and I am about to cater Andolini's first wedding. It's a simple enough order, mostly pasta, for a wedding fifteen miles west into farm country at a barn. A nice barn. The kind of barn you have a wedding at.

I'm standing in the middle of my restaurant. My catering order is getting put into delivery bags. The pans of pasta are getting foil lids placed on them, my car is out back, and I'm ten minutes from when I need to leave to arrive at the barn on time. It's 6 p.m. on a Saturday, and I'm about to be away from my restaurant for ninety minutes. I will have eight employees in my restaurant without a manager for these ninety minutes—a dumb thing I wouldn't do today.

In my head, all I can think over and over is, "What has gone wrong? What is not right? What else needs to be done? What have I forgotten? What have I forgotten? What have I forgotten? Double-check the order. Check off that we have every item. Double-check it again. Do I have a pen because I'm going to need them to sign the credit card receipt? Hold on. What bride will want to sign for a credit card receipt ten minutes before their wedding? Do I need someone else to go with me to this thing? Oh shit, I don't have anyone else that could go with me to this thing. All right. This order is going to be OK. I need to get this order to be OK. Just get there early. Bag it up. Get on the road already."

While I'm thinking to myself what I need to do, I'm not in a state of panic or doubt. I'm in a state of self-evaluation that I am not perfect, and I surely got something wrong here, and no matter how many times I go over it in my head, it is not going to hurt me. The only thing that can hurt me is forgetting something and fucking up this wedding and someone's special day. I need this order to be perfect. I need this order to go well so they recommend us to other people and also so I can pay myself this week.

That's the world I lived in then. That's the mindset and world I still live in today. Continually asking, "What is wrong?" gives me the ability to find out what's right or what could be better. If I had the thought, "I'm great, and this wedding is lucky to have me bring the food.

Everything's fine enough. No one's going to have a problem, and if someone does have a problem, well, we're
the best pizza, so who is going to mind that much?"

That's an egotistical and naive approach to this business. It's also a common approach to this business; far
more common than you would think. As I have stated
multiple times, your ego is worthless. Your love of your
reputation gives you nothing towards your future. It's
the enemy of your future.

You have to embrace that you potentially suck.

That your pizza might not be that great, that your
sauce could have more flavor, and your flour mix might
be weak. The cheese you're buying, even if it's the most
expensive, might not be the best choice for your end
product. To know that even if you purchased everything right and showed the recipe perfectly, your staff
might cook it wrong.

Assuming your food quality isn't an issue, what if the
servers suck. What about the ambiance, are these lights
and your fixtures helping the brand? Take all that off the
table; is your marketing crap?

Asking, "Do I suck?" helps you find reasons you do,
and then, even better, how you can fix those things.
Everything can be better. The sooner you realize this
and create systems that ensure you get better, the sooner
you grow and become more profitable. Complacency

and happiness are garbage feelings with a restaurant. I can't reiterate it enough. *The happiness and complacency of today is the direct enemy of your tomorrow.*

I will repeat:

The happiness and complacency of today is the direct enemy of your tomorrow.

If you've never been in awe of another restaurant, then you are too in love with your own restaurant. I am in awe of other restaurants all the time. Maybe just one aspect of it, but I'm in awe, and that awe makes me want to reevaluate my status of how I'm approaching that issue, be it the food, the service, or the ambiance, or any subset of either. Being in awe means there's something I haven't thought of, which again, makes me better. I'm never jealous of other's success to think something like, "Man, we deserve to have that," or, "It's bullshit that they have that much business," because jealousy is a wasted emotion. It gains you nothing. My Mom Marge drilled that in my head at a young age. "If you're mad that someone else has something better than you, either get over it or figure out how to get it yourself because the jealousy is a wasted emotion."

There is a world of information and resources you have yet to tap. For example, I love music. I listened to a lot of music in high school, as much music as I could get my hands on, which before the rise of Napster and iTunes, wasn't that easy. There was no Spotify for me in high school, just whatever was on the radio and MTV. If I heard a song I liked, I had to scrounge up money to afford the CD to listen to it more than randomly on the radio. In high school, my friend Dan gave me a CD and said, "If you like Metallica, you have to listen to this. It's the Misfits," I said, "OK, cool." He said, "No. You'll love this album, and you'll never hear this shit on the radio. There are thousands of albums you'll never be force-fed by radio that you would dig if you had the album." He made me a list of albums to listen to. He also said, "You gotta find shit that's unique to you." It opened my eyes to how much beyond radio there was to hear. I wondered how many great movies there were beyond what was on TV. I became fascinated by how many great books I wasn't reading beyond what we were forced to read at school. Before the age of information, I was an info junkie. Today, it's impossible to take in all the content available to us. Today, it's hard to decipher what's worth your mental real estate. For me today, I try to listen to a variety of podcasts and music when I drive from store to store. I try to read as much as time will allow. There is so much more knowledge to be gained, that the second you think you've heard, or in this case, seen, it all, you handicap yourself.

Case in point, in 2013, I proposed to my then-girl-friend, who became my fiancé, and is now my wife. After we got engaged, we went to a wedding show at a hotel ballroom. At this wedding show was your standard wedding booths with DJs, tux rentals, photography, and what I was very surprised to see so little of, catering. There were two booths for catering. They were both businesses that *only* did catering and were not brick and mortar restaurants. At that moment I thought, "I've done weddings, but I've never done a wedding show, and these two catering companies aren't doing anything I can't do. I can probably do what they do."

That's confidence, not cockiness, because to deliver on that promise takes the ingenuity to say, "Everything I'd been doing up to this point has been done, and I haven't thought to do this yet." I found the cost to get a booth at the next wedding show. It wasn't that expensive at six hundred bucks. We signed up 150 brides to do a dinner tasting and ended up doing tastings for fifty brides, thirty-five of which turned into weddings, that's thirty-five weddings, which turned into about $100,000 in new sales, just for my six hundred dollar investment. At that point, I completely re-engineered the game of what we did as a pizzeria to increase our wedding catering exposure. It's now one of the cornerstones of Andolini's profit streams. That started from the thought, "Is there something else we're not doing?" Sure as shit there is. There always is.

The Marine Corps makes it painfully evident there is always something more you aren't considering. When tasked with cleaning something as simple as our barracks, mostly metal, and linoleum, there's seemingly an endless number of nooks and crannies to clean. Some of the OCS candidates had already gone to regular enlisted boot camp, so now at OCS to become officers, they knew what to prepare for. We cleaned above and inside the fluorescent lights. We unscrewed the showerhead to wash behind it. Still, the Platoon Sergeants would find something wrong and then would make our fuck up abundantly clear to the platoon.

I was given a billet of being the Commanding Officer of my platoon for two days. I devised a plan to win "The Glorious 8 Seconds." Just like riding a bull, my main goal, with drill instructors abound, would be to get eight seconds where no Platoon Sergeant could find something that we as a platoon had not cleaned. I said this to the platoon, "I'm tired as fuck of being called out for shit after working my balls off. I know now, just like all of you know, they're going to create something if they can't find something. Our goal is to go eight seconds without these bastard fucks finding anything on us. Who else is game?" We cleaned the hell out of the barracks, more than we had ever done before.

When inspection time came, the Platoon Sergeant looked at the showerhead, the lights, opened a few lockers, checked the dust above the locker, and then walked down the barracks. I motioned with my fingers a count of one, two, three, four... the other candidates saw my hand through the corner of their eyes, six, seven, eight, nine seconds. Then the Platoon Sergeant said, "You dickheads think you're hot shit, don't you? Well, these windows out here look like garbage." He then went into the stairwell and pointed out the exterior of the fifth-floor barracks' windows' dust. We had done it. We got our eight seconds, and we all knew it. Later that night, a separate DI, Sergeant Hernandez, an angry, super heavy Marine who had never relented on me at any point, said in passing, "Bausch, if you can find a way to do that shit with Marines, you'll be fucking fine. Now get the fuck away from me."

That compliment came after weeks of what felt like failures. It was a big deal for me and a morale booster. I had all fifty members of my platoon rallying to get those eight seconds. The drill instructor's best recourse to criticize us was to point out the dirt on the exterior window of our fifth-floor barracks stairwell. We would've needed a fifty-foot ladder to get to that. But he hadn't come up with that. The best he could come up with was something outside our barracks. That gave me and the platoon a lot of confidence, but it also showed me that there's always something else. There's *always* something else.

You are missing out on revenue right now.

There are more monetary opportunities you have yet to tap. If you're doing everything right and there's nothing else to do, then why are you still reading this book? If you want to find the money you are missing, go after the things you would not usually choose. Choose events or groups of people you have never been around and meet them. If you've never been to a rodeo, ask to cater one. If you only feed the local high school, go to the colleges. If you hate dance moms, then...well, that's probably for the best.

Realizing that you're not the best and that there's more to do is strength. When you ask yourself, "What did I forget? What did I forget? What did I forget? What did I forget?" like an insane person, you find out what you might've forgotten or never even thought of in the first place. Humility gets us to that point. Being humble is a direct tie to any success I've ever had. Any outward self-endorsement is for marketing or to inform, never to brag. I'm a believer that successful people who seem egotistical are always self-evaluating, and their braggadocio is fake. Like Rick Flair yelling out a "Woo" before taking on Dusty Rhodes, it's all an act. Knowing you don't know everything is an advantage.

THE JERK, THE SLEAZE, AND THE IDIOT

Think about every reality TV restaurant show you've ever seen. You know the ones, where they fix up a failing bar or restaurant in a minimal amount of time. Let's take Bar Rescue with Jon Taffer, for example. Each episode falls into three distinct categories of the person being rescued. They're either a jerk, a sleaze, or an idiot. Again, a jerk, a sleaze, or an idiot.

The Jerk

The jerk yells at their staff indiscriminately. They take their aggression out on staff without reason. These are owners so frustrated with life, they assume yelling at people into submission will lead to results. They're wrong, and life beats them over the head, or the person running the restaurant repair show does. This example of a crappy restaurateur is someone needing therapy or something to fix their life. A restaurant is not the answer.

The Sleaze

The sleaze doesn't pay their staff. The sleaze will say and do dirty things around members of the opposite sex and is a generally creepy person. This person also shouldn't get their whole restaurant super fixed-up for free, but they do make for good TV. Can they be fixed? Most likely not unless they do a full 180 on their morality.

The Idiot!!! *Yay!!!!!!!!!!!!!*

Last and certainly not least is the idiot. The idiot is the best version of what you want to see on a mission impossible style restaurant show. The idiot is someone with an absence of knowledge. They are someone who's in over their heads and has no idea and is looking for a life preserver. This person can accept teaching and training. This person admits they don't know it all, and they're trying and hoping for someone to help them figure it out. Being an idiot and realizing it is the first step on your path to knowledge. Once that is settled, the fixer can do their job, adjust their skillset, and teach them what to do correctly from a solid base.

So gloriously declare yourself an idiot and go forth hoping to fix that which you don't know. Saying, "Never again will I let this happen," lets you create progress. Progress enables you to build systems that support a strong foundation—a strong foundation that bypasses idiotic actions in the future.

FOR THIS AUDITORY PALATE CLEANSER

Jack White has an ability to fuse country, rock, and blues without sounding like he's paying homage, but instead that he's on par and surpassing those he emulates. This song has several interpretations; the most common is a story of a child who's jealous of a new sibling. The anxiety-ridden pace and beat of the thump remind me of putting in work. True work: the kind of tireless work you do when you think you're done, and you have to do it again. This next chapter is about getting tasks that annoy the shit out of you systematically accomplished.

Please enjoy,

"The Hardest Button to Button"
by The White Stripes

CHAPTER 8

CREATE MILLION DOLLAR SYSTEMS

For anything that annoys you that could be better, make a system. This chapter will detail how to do that so it allows you to go home and know everything will be OK. Systems need repetition. Systems take time and money to create. Remember, for the hundreds of dollars they cost to create, they save thousands, which turn into millions. They also create millions when it's a profit generator systemized properly. Systems assume you are not in love with the current state of affairs to the point that you are opposed to progress. Many people hate progress as it is uncomfortable.

There's a parable story I tell my staff. I heard this once in a restaurant and it always stuck with me. A family on Christmas day had their littlest granddaughter ask her mother a question. She asked why every year on

Christmas, they cut the four corners off the ham they bake for dinner. The Mom said, "Because that's how you cook a ham. You cut the corners off it before you bake it." The little girl insisted, "But why do you do it?" The Mother retorted, "Well, that's how we've always done it. You can even ask your grandmother." The little girl then says to her Grandma, "Grandma, why do we cut the four corners of the ham off before we bake it?"

Grandma then says, "Well, that's how you cook ham, honey." "But why?" the little girl frustratingly said. The little girl then looked to her Great-Grandma and asked, "Great-Grandma, why do we cut the corners off this ham?" And the Great-Grandma said, "Well in the 1940s I had a very small oven. So, to fit the ham into our small oven, I cut the corners so the ham would fit in the pan."

The fact that something's done one way for a long period does not mean it is the correct way to do it.

People believe, especially in the pizza industry, that you need to do things in a very specific way or else you're wrong. If they have that reasoning based on and rooted in science, great. Typically, it's not rooted in the science of baking or fermentation. Typically, it's not rooted in putting the customer first. More often than not, it's rooted in superstition that there's one way it should be done and to not rock the boat.

Gleaning knowledge from someone else's process is sound logic. Basing a business off monkey-see monkey-do is foolish. That's how jorts became popular. Remember jean shorts, the fashion trend predicated on the questions, "Do you love jeans? Ever wish you could wear jeans in the summer?" That was bad, and it became a super popular fashion trend when one idiot imitated another idiot. For any problem in your business, there's a solution. All solutions need a system to maintain that solution. All systems must be tested, evaluated, and retested for it to last over time. And the testing must be evaluated regularly. Do not keep doing something wrong forever because that's the way you've always seen it done. Instead, create systems and fix the problems that cost you money. Always ask, "Is there a smarter way to do this?" Never be in love with the past. Create and use your system in perpetuity until you revise it again.

WE CAN DO THAT

Remember the basic leadership plan. Assess your situation and then create a system. Then explain the system and execute. If something goes wrong, reassess and fix it. Then try it all again. For any task on your plate, know this to be true. If it can be done, you can learn how to do it. Once you know, then you can take action and fix it. Personally, I don't like the term DIY (do it yourself). I mean, I'm a big do-it-yourselfer, but I prefer WCDT (we can do that). We've said that a lot in our business.

Take a regular task like pizza oven maintenance. We've stayed up all night when the oven technician came to town, just to watch him work. We filmed what he did and worked with him throughout the night. The technician even said this was atypical of most restaurant owners. Fast-forward to the next time the oven went down, we knew exactly what to do and were back up in minutes instead of days.

At our first store, we had a grease trap filled with the sludge that comes from the dish machine. It was an above-ground liquid compost that a grease company would come to empty. They would take a big hose and suck it all away into their septic truck.

It cost a bunch of money each time they came, so I figured a way to do it with a shop vac and avoided the weekly fee. When we only had dollars to get by on, this was a big deal.

Instead of paying a service to hand out door hangers to residential areas, I did it. Also, door hangers are antiquated now, but pre-Facebook it was the name of the game. Once I saw their return rate, I created shifts of workers to do this as well to cover more area. Servers were dependable door hanger staff because they benefited from the result of more diners. We didn't pay someone else hundreds for something they had no stake in; instead, we thought: we can do that.

Eventually, we figured out exactly where we needed to deliver to and how often. We then trained a Boy Scout troop to do it. They could do it in the way we knew worked best. In turn, we fed them in pizza parties and service badges, not dollars.

If it's not something that you need to do, you can teach someone else to do it. If it's not for your company to do, you can outsource it. Outsource it when you 100% know how to do it yourself. Only then can you intelligently know the cost of it vs. the cost of your time.

MEASURE IT

For anything that you do, you need to measure it because that which is measured, gets done. For example, don't buy park bench ad space with your whole marketing budget and call it a day. You put a code on an item to make sure it's part of a system where you can track and follow the code. That's pizza redemption 101. With online ads, it has become harder and easier to achieve this, depending on how you set up the ad or coupon.

Every system with a measurement to determine ROI will prove if it's worth reinvesting in. Another example of a system that every single restaurant will need to do is a closeout sheet. A closeout sheet should be a simple system. A proper sheet is an absolute mandate for any successful pizzeria. You need a closeout sheet for FOH and one for BOH. Here are three fairly simple FOH tasks; roll silverware, clean the bathrooms, and wipe the menus. If you assume staff will automatically do tasks, you'll have one person out of twenty actually do it. The person that does do it will be because they're a clean freak. Then you'll ask, "How come everyone doesn't do it? How come everyone can't be as good as this one person?"

The reason is this person is exceptional, and your system did not proactively plan for the normal worker. The true problem is you didn't measure it. You hoped that it would get done. To ensure things get done, you need a closeout list that gets checked daily. You could make a perfect ideal list of tasks, but if there is no system tied to it, it will never get filled out.

The manager on duty has to see the completed list before the person tasked with filling it out can leave. Otherwise, it will never get taken seriously over time and they're going to do it a few days and give up on it. In reality, it needs to be the ticket to go home, "I've turned in my closeout sheet; can I go?"

YOU MUST INSPECT, NOT EXPECT

But the goal is not to have sheets turned in; the goal is to have a clean restaurant. If the MOD doesn't inspect what's on the sheet, staff will turn in half-assed sheets. These sheets will have tasks checked off that didn't get accomplished. The goal is a clean restaurant. Thus, you have to *inspect*, not *expect* that things get done correctly. The second you expect and assume things are done correctly, i.e., set it and forget it, that's when everything goes to shit.

You can make the most glorious system ever, but it's worthless without a DRI. If a manager says to staff, "Hey, everyone, roll silverware tonight at some point." Then one person's going to roll a few rolls, and so will a few other members of staff. When tomorrow shows that not enough was rolled, staff will play the blame game of who didn't do their part. They'll point fingers with no knowledge of who is actually at fault. The true person at fault is the manager who gave vague directions. This has to be a specific system. For example, the first server to get cut rolls a hundred rolls of silverware. Once done, check it off your checklist and turn in your sheet to be allowed to clock off. This way, it's clear, concise, and direct. Now you'll know that the first person cut, i.e., Tom, is now responsible for this task. But how will you maintain people valuing the system over individual extenuating circumstances?

STAFF MUST ADHERE TO THE STANDARD (NOT STANDARDS CONFORMING TO STAFF)

Standards should not override judgment, extenuating circumstances will arise, and leadership should prevail. Invoices turned in by 9 a.m. can't adjust for someone who doesn't like to come in on Mondays. Yet invoices turned in by 9 a.m. can adjust one time for someone with a family member in the hospital. The rules having *some* leeway is vital; consistent leeway makes it a worthless rule.

And people can't be more important than standards because people leave. People quit, transfer, upgrade, and downgrade. When the system depends on people instead of standards, the system is unreliable. The person depended upon is a keystone, strong when there, a crumbled pile when they leave. Avoid this with checks and balances. All systems need backups, and all roles necessitate cross-training. For example, if only one person has access to all the passwords of your company, then without someone else knowing how to access them, you are set up for failure if that person ever becomes incapacitated.

In that simple but technologically relevant issue, a password manager tool with backup security protocols is critical. That way other people can act in their place if that person can't work, but you still maintain security. A protocol where an individual can be removed, and that person can't see the passwords anymore is vital to business. That's how you maintain non-keystone systems.

Someone is a keystone liability when you can't quickly answer this question; "If that person dies tomorrow, what would we need to do?" If it's not moving these responsibilities over to that other person, and train them on it, then as a backup plan it is worthless. All roles must be documented and disclosed. It should be evident to the officers of your company who has access to what and what parts they are responsible for conducting. Additionally, who is their backup for each role? Otherwise, the system is set up for failure because everyone will peel off, including you at some point, when you might be sick or out of pocket unexpectedly. If you haven't planned for that situation, you haven't taken care of your business. You're taking care of today; you're not taking care of tomorrow. And tomorrow is as important, if not more, than today. To do otherwise is as foolish as Velcro logic.

Velcro Logic

Imagine an employee in your restaurant tripped on their shoelaces and fell. Then instead of telling all your employees to make sure to tie their shoes, you said, "Everyone from now on must only wear Velcro shoes at work." That would be dumb, right? However, businesses often cater to the lowest common denominator instead of eliminating it. I'm all for easy-to-follow rules, but I also encourage an environment of using your head. I'm not suggesting you assume your staff members are Mensa geniuses. At the same time, don't talk down to them in a way that assumes everyone is an idiot. If you do, they will reward you by proving you correct and acting like idiots; with someone who doesn't use common sense, establish that it's unacceptable. The next step is to build a culture that encourages a "figure it out" mentality and doesn't accept mediocrity.

Government agencies often use Velcro logic, as you see at the DMV. Stupid systems that assume everyone who works there is a cog and nothing more. You own an independent restaurant built on ingenuity and logic, so expect your staff to show the same traits.

I have a friend who owns a bakery that sells baked goods to grocery stores. He's evaluated on a very high level by many governmental organizations. When he sought USDA certification, the amount of bureaucracy he dealt with was beyond exasperating. They demand high standards of cleanliness, as they should. But on a recent inspection, he was noted as in violation for having silicone caulking in a toolbox. His safety score took a hit. The inspector said unsecured silicone caulking was a potentially dangerous hazard. They said, "It could end up in his cream-filled donuts. It could happen by accident or on purpose by an angry employee." My friend said, "That's crazy." The inspector said, "Well, it happened once, so now it's a rule."

Instead of the USDA dealing with that instance of crime alone, now all bakeries need to modify their protocols. If my friend wants silicone caulking on-premise, it must be in a locked facility only he can access. It must also be nowhere near the production floor. This rule was not an outlier but rather one of several regulations he had never heard before that were now his mandate.

Make rules that establish order. Remember, if you make too many rules, no one's going to abide. If there are so many rules that no one can remember them, or they are egregious, then the rules aren't valued. If the speed limit was ten miles above what it is now, would everyone go twenty miles above what they do now? I don't think they would. Speed limits are typically lower, assuming people will go slightly above them. Most cops don't ticket unless you're far above the speed limit, i.e., the speed limit is a loose rule. *Don't make loose rules.* Make fair rules that everyone can abide by, and if they are not abided by, will not be tolerated per the standard. My most successful restaurant focused rule that must be a mandate is the prep list. It's the backbone of knowing what is done and what needs to be done. I achieve this via a whiteboard system.

The Whiteboard

Some restaurants do their prep and closeout sheets on paper. Some do them on laminated pages on clipboards. Over time digital lists have become more popular. I've found all these solutions work but are not clearly visible. As a result, their effectiveness starts to wane over time.

To ensure tasks get done, I use a large whiteboard in my restaurants. It has every task that needs to get done by day and night crews. It clarifies tasks to all staff. With a proper whiteboard, any server could view the BOH

DAY: M T W Th F Sa Sn

ANDOLINI'S
EST. INCORPORATED 2005

INITIAL ALL DONE TASKS

DOUGH

Item	Have	M-T min/max	F-Sn min/max	Prep	Done
4oz					
8oz					
14oz					
20oz					
28oz					
Knots					

PIZZA PREP

Item	Have	M-T min/max	F-Sn min/max	Prep	Done
PIZZA SAUCE					
MOZZ BINS					
PASTRAMI					
SLICED SAUSAGE					
SALAMI					
HAMBURGER					
IT SAUSAGE					
CANADIAN BACON					
CHICKEN DICED					
PANCETTA					
SPECK					
PROSCIUTTO					
WHOLE MILK MOZZ					
SMOKED MOZZ					
SHRED PARM					

SHIFT NOTES

SKILL

Item	Have	M-T min/max	F-Sn min/max	Prep	Done
BBQ SAUCE					
FRESH MOZZ					
IT SAUSAGE					
CHICKEN					
MEAT MIX					
MEATBALL TRAY					
GF DOUGH					
PASTRAMI					
PORCHETTA					
( )					
( )					

SLICER

Item	Have	M-T min/max	F-Sn min/max	Prep	Done
GREEN BELLS					
PANCETTA					
PASTRAMI					
PEPPERONI					
PORCHETTA					
PROSCIUTTO					
RED ONIONS					
SALAMI					
TOMATOES					
SMOKED MOZZ					
SPECK					
EGGPLANT					

OVEN CLEAN

Week 1: Windows & Inside ___
Week 2: Windows & Below ___
Week 3: Windows & FanVent ___
Week 4: Windows & Above ___

COOK SIDE PREP

Item	Have	M-T min/max	F-Sn min/max	Prep	Done
BASIL					
GRATED PEC					
MOZZARO BELLS					
ARTICHOKES					
MEAT SAUCE					
MINCED GARLIC					
PESTO					
SLICED BREAD					
ROASTED GARLIC					
DICED TOMATOES					
CAESAR					
ITALIAN					
MANGO					
RANCH					
SAN MARZANO					
BALSAMIC VIN					
ORANGE VIN					
GORGONZOLA					
HONEY VIN					

DAILY CLEAN

Monday: Hood Vents ___
Tuesday: Stove Detail ___
Wednesday: Roto-Flex Work (one night) ___
Thursday: Behind Cook Line ___
Friday: ( ) ___
Saturday: ( ) ___
Sunday: Dry Storage ___

WEEKLY CLEAN

WEEK 1: CONVECTION OVEN DETAIL ___
WEEK 2: WALK IN DETAIL ___
WEEK 3: WALL DETAIL ___
WEEK 4: CEILING LIGHT VENTS ___

MONTHLY CLEAN

Jan: Vents ___ July: Vents ___
Feb: Fridge Fans ___ Aug: Fridge Fans ___
March: Pots Disks ___ Sept: Pots Disks ___
April: Vents ___ Oct: Vents ___
May: Fridge Fans ___ Nov: Fridge Fans ___
June: Pots Disks ___ Dec: Pots Disks ___

PRE-CLOSE CLEAN

BINS CHANGED OUT: ___
MATS: ___
PIZZA STATION CLEAN: ___
( ): ___

POST-CLOSE

ALL LEVELS WIPED: ___
ALL ITEMS TO DISH: ___
ALL EQUIPMENT OFF: ___
FLOORS SCRUBBED: ___
PRODUCE ORDERED: ___
ALL LIGHTS OFF: ___

SLICE SCHEDULE

Monday: _____
Tuesday: _____
Wednesday: _____
Thursday: _____
Friday: _____

PM PRE-CHECK

URGENT ITEMS CIRCLE: ___
ALL PARS DOUBLE CHECKED: ___
GOOD TO GO FOR PM SERVICE: ___

NOTES

BOH prep board

whiteboard and know if all tasks for today are complete. It would be apparent via the initials next to every task that the crew is ready for the next rush.

If a task gets initialed complete when it wasn't actually done, it's a fireable offense. Why? Because if the

ANDOLINI'S EST INCORPORATED 1986

DAY: M T W Th F Sa Sn

INITIAL ALL DONE TASKS

SERVER AM TASKS
- SET UP PATIO ___ FILL SANI BUCKETS ___
- BATHROOM FULL CLEAN ___ EMPTY TRASH & LINENS ___
- FILL ICE (WIPE FIRST) ___ ROLL REMAINING SILVERWARE ___
- STOCK DISHES ___ SECTION STAGED ___
- STOCK TO GO ITEMS ___ ORGANIZE STORAGE ___
- SWEEP ALL ___ FILL CARAFES ___
- GELATO CASE ___ SWEEP PATIO ___
- GELATO SPADES ___

HOST AM TASKS
- SWEEP ENTRY ___ CLEAN WINDOWS ___
- SWEEP HOST ___ ORGANIZE HOST STAND ___
- SECTIONS MADE ___ UNLOCK DOOR @11AM ___
- FILL SANI BUCKET ___ TURN ON OPEN SIGN ___

HOST PM CLOSE
- SWEEP ENTRY ___ CLEAN WINDOWS ___
- SWEEP HOST ___ ORGANIZE HOST STAND ___
- CHARGE IPAD ___ CLEAN ALL KID CHAIRS ___
- CHANGE SANIBUCKET ___ CHANGE HOST TRASH ___

SERVER 1ST CUT
- FOLD __ 16oz BOXES ___ WIPE PIZZA STANDS ___
- FILL ICE (LUNCH) ___ STOCK PLATES&GLASSES ___
- ROLL __ ROLLUPS ___ SWEEP SECTION ___

SERVER 6TH CUT
- EMPTY & REMOVE TRASH ___ WIPE PIZZA STAND ___
- CLEAN SERVER TRAYS ___ STOCK PLATES&GLASSES ___
- ROLL __ ROLLUPS ___ SWEEP SECTION ___

SERVER 2ND CUT
- FOLD __ 20in BOXES ___ WIPE PIZZA STANDS ___
- SANI BUCKETS (LUNCH) ___ STOCK PLATES&GLASSES ___
- ROLL __ ROLLUPS ___ SWEEP SECTION ___

SERVER 7TH CUT
- POLISH & STOCK SPOONS ___ WIPE PIZZA STAND ___
- POLISH OTHER SILVERWARE ___ STOCK PLATES&GLASSES ___
- ROLL __ ROLLUPS ___ SWEEP SECTION ___

SERVER 3RD CUT
- FOLD __ 14in BOXES ___ WIPE PIZZA STANDS ___
- ROLL __ ROLLUPS ___ STOCK PLATES&GLASSES ___
- STOCK SPATULAS ___ SWEEP SECTION ___

SERVER 4TH CUT
- STOCK BATHROOM ___ WIPE PIZZA STANDS ___
- CLEAN BATHROOMS ___ STOCK PLATES&GLASSES ___
- ROLL __ ROLLUPS ___ SWEEP SECTION ___

SERVER 5TH CUT
- CLEAN CHECK PRESENTERS ___ STOCK CLEAN SERVER STATIONS ___
- ROLL __ ROLLUPS ___ STOCK PLATES&GLASSES ___
- SWEEP SECTION ___

FOH CLOSER
- SERVERS CHECKED OUT ___ CLEAN/TO GO STATION ___
- EMPTY CARAFES ___ FLOORS MOPPED ___
- EMPTY SANI BUCKETS ___ CLEAN EXPO LINE ___
- ROLL UP FROM ROLLUPS ___ EMPTY ANY OTHER TRASH ___
- CLOSER IS RESPONSIBLE FOR DELEGATING ANY CLOSING DUTIES NOT ASSIGNED WHEN THERE ARE LESS CLOSERS THAN LISTED!

BAR AM / BAR CLOSE
- CUT LEMONS TO BAR ___ CARAFES TO DISH ___
- STOCK BOTTLE COOLER ___ TEA& COFFEE TO DISH ___
- MAKE TEA/COFFEE ___ SODA GUNS IN SANITIZER ___
- STOCK WINE ___ BAR TOP WIPED ___
- MOP BAR FLOOR ___ ALL BAR TOOLS TO DISH ___
- COVER TAPS/BOTTLES ___
- BAR MATS TO DISH ___
- PERISHABLE TO DISH ___
- BURN BAR ICE BIN ___

AM PREP
Item I Have | M.T | F.Sn | Prep I Done
(mañana | mañana)
- LEMONS ___
- Roll Ups ___
- 14in BOXES ___
- 14in BOXES ___
- 16in BOXES ___
- 20in BOXES ___

AM SHIFT CHANGE
- EMPTY TRASH ___ BATHROOMS CLEAN ___
- EMPTY LINEN ___ BATHROOMS STOCKED ___
- EMPTY TOWEL ___ STOCK TO GO ITEMS ___
- STOCK DISHES ___ SWEEP FOH ___

PM SERVER CLOSING
- SECTIONS CLEAN ___ BATHROOMS CLEAN ___
- EMPTY LINEN ___ STOCK TO GO ITEMS ___
- EMPTY TOWEL ___ STOCK TO GO ITEMS ___
- STOCK DISHES ___ FLOORS SWEPT ___
- PATIO/OUTSIDE ___ SILVERWARE ___
- GELATO CASE ___ GELATO AREA ___

DAILY FOH CLEAN
- MON: DEEP CLEAN UNDER TABLE TOP
- TUES: OREGANO SHAKERS (DUMP & RUN THRU DISH)
- WED: RED PEPER SHAKERS (DUMP & RUN THRU DISH)
- THURS: DUST ALL FRAMES & PICS
- FRI: FILL SALT& PEPPER SHAKERS
- SAT: DUST LIGHTS & FANS & SHELVES
- SUN: DECK BRUSH FLOORS (HIGH TRAFFIC & ENTRANCES AS WELL)

DAILY BAR CLEAN
- MON: GLASS RACKS & MATS
- TUES: HIGHER UP SHELVES DUSTED AND WIPED
- WED: BEHIND COOLERS CLEANED
- THURS: CLEAN FLOOR DRAINS
- FRI: SPOUTS&COVERS TO DISH
- SAT: CLEAN TAP WALL & FAUCETS
- SUN: DETAIL ALL SPOUTS & GUNS

FOH prep board

system has loose rules, then it's worthless. Worthless systems destroy restaurants.

The whiteboard is a simple idea I saw when I was visiting my Mom in the hospital. What I saw in this place where people live and die based upon doctors' decisions was simple and obvious. Their communication tool was a whiteboard with the patients' pertinent info. There was no way to confuse the patient's info this way. And the patient could circle which emoji of how they were feeling. I realized at that moment you can print anything into a dry-erase board. I took the shit sandwich of my Mom being ill at the hospital and learned something from another industry. I told her the idea and she said, "That makes a lot of sense. At least you got something out of me being in here." As if visiting your Mom in the hospital is a waste.

That idea became something I ran with and whiteboards are in all our stores. It's a communication tool, it's a management tool. It's just a simple ass system that works. For any task, prep item, daily, weekly, or yearly cleaning task, the whiteboard is the answer. My example is below; you can make this yourself and get staff all on the same page. The whiteboard tells people what needs to be prepped. It maintains pars. When people over prep and go order past your pars, you have food waste. When that occurs, you have to apply toothpaste logic to your pars and staff.

Toothpaste Logic

You know that last bit of toothpaste. It's the little bit that keeps on giving. It's incredible the amount of toothpaste you can scrape out of a tube when you have no more tubes available. Remember that feeling of fighting to get it all out when you are too poor to buy more? That is the value of appreciating running low on something and valuing every ounce of it. Inversely, when you have an abundance of toothpaste, you become wasteful. Like you went to Costco and bought the super pack and now you can make it rain toothpaste in the club if you so choose. Around three-fourths deep into that tube, you think, "A nice, new full tube would look better on my counter." The same mindset happens in restaurants. When you've over-purchased, people waste significantly more.

You need to ride the line tight, and that means things will run out occasionally. It also means that your food costs will be tight and that you'll have the freshest product possible. Don't underbuy items like flour or mozzarella but be smarter with your purchasing. Apply toothpaste logic to your daily ops. Waste management requires a team effort. It's hard to make running tight food cost a win for everyone other than you, the person paying the bills. Staff needs motivation to become waste hawks. They need a win or loss to have their ass in the game like you, the owner, does. We fought and tried for years to accomplish this, and we finally did in 2018 with the Feast or Famine program.

Feast or Famine

Here's another system that we invented for Andolini's. Necessity was the mother of this invention. Staff was not motivated to hit food cost. This system solved that. The food cost metrics you decide on should match your targeted goal. As I said before, ours is 30% or less, but depending on your restaurant, yours could be different. We decided to lay it out and say no more discounted meals for employees. But, if you hit your targeted numbers, you eat for free (feast).

Conversely, if you don't hit your targeted numbers, you get absolutely nothing (famine). It was a ballsy gamble that has paid off. When staff has their ass on the line with you, they act as such. Here is how it works. Below is verbatim what we put in front of the employees during training.

Free Employee Food

If your store hits 30% or less on food cost, you get to eat *anything you want. YES, ANYTHING!*

Food cost is calculated on a Monday—Sunday basis and is posted Tuesday morning. If

your store hits 30% or less, then free food
to you until next Tuesday's posting.

Free food applies before or after any shift you
have, and you can request anything you'd want
to try. Just have a manager send in the order and
approve it. You must eat it on-site and can't take
it to go or use any to-go packaging materials.

In Addition to That
Don't want to eat before or after work,
but want to have Andolini's on days you
don't work? Any to-go order is 20% off for
employees if your store is at 30% or less.

Any dine-in order (not including alcohol) is 50% off for you and up to 3 guests,
if your store is at 30% or less.

Feast or Famine has yielded wonders. We kept saying, "These guys don't get that when they fuck this up,
it screws up cash flow; how do we get them to care as
much as we do?" Feast or Famine did that. If a manager or any employee violates the rule, it is immediately
fireable. The staff wants to eat our food. That's good
because it means they're excited about their job. It's
good for us, too, because we want staff to eat their way
through the menu, on us. Speaking of menus...

Keeping things fresh in a restaurant means new items, but adding a menu item is an undertaking. Here is a detailed process with high specificity to ensure the roll-out of any new menu item goes smoothly.

PATHWAY TO A MENU ITEM

I created a checklist I reference every time I am about to introduce a new menu item. It has everything I'll need to do in advance of launching the menu item. I've perfected it over the years.

I never introduce a new menu item without going right back to this list and making sure I check off every task. Even though I've been doing this for sixteen years, I still always look at the path to a menu item list. Sometimes I realize, "Hey, I missed one aspect of it," or, "I should add this note to the path." Whatever new thing I notice, I add it to that list. Adding third-party delivery menu updates to the list was my latest addition. This way, I have a reference point for the future.

Here is my eighteen-step path to a menu item (I know, eighteen is a lot; it was once nine, but I found I kept forgetting important stuff):

1. New Item Conceptualized

You've dreamt up a new item and tried it yourself, tasted it, and believe it deserves a place on your menu.

2. Tested and Agreed On

You then have other people try the item. People who don't care about hurting your feelings. Not friends and family but more so foodies and people whose palate you respect. And give the item to kitchen staff and servers to get their unique take. Clarify that being honest and even negative is not only OK but encouraged. Make sure the item has an execution time that fits into your service time standards. Cross-utilize existing ingredients before introducing new ones into your kitchen. Ingredients that are not cross-utilized lead to disorganized kitchens and waste.

3. Process Created

Decide the process of this new item. Choose where on the make line to hold the new ingredients. Decide how many ounces, cups, or slices of product will go into this item per the recipe.

4. In-House Menu, Description, and Price Finite

Decide the name, the story, and verbiage for the item along with the price. The price should be determined based on three factors. What it costs to make, what the market already charges for like items, and most importantly, how much you can charge for it once marketed well. Sometimes start soft on price and increase once demand grows. Never start an item off with a lousy food cost to get it to sell. If you do that, you're selling for the price rather than the product. That's a recipe for disaster.

5. Excel Recipe Shot and Made

Make a recipe card you can give to anyone that makes it clear how to prepare this item the right way. It should be very specific with pictures and clear directions.

6. Marketing Photos Made of New Items

Hire a pro or learn how to become a pro with high-resolution shots that entice hunger. If you haven't taken photography classes or have a portfolio of successful photos, don't do this. Great photos pay for themselves quickly, three hundred to five hundred dollars is a good range for a ninety-minute photoshoot with enhancements to final edits. Adjust for inflation for whatever year after 2020 you're reading this, but anything more than that is photog hubris.

7. Modify the Order Guide

If new ingredients are added to your kitchen, you need to source them and add them to your order guide.

CUSTOM - CHEESE PIZZA BASE		14in	16in	20in
STEP 1	PIZZA SAUCE	Spoodle	1	2	3
STEP 2	MOZZARELLA - DICED	OZ	7	9	17
STEP 3	EXT CHEESE / CUSTOM PLAIN	OZ	9	12	20
BAKE IN OVEN				
PECORINO EXPO		Tblsp	1	1 1/2	2

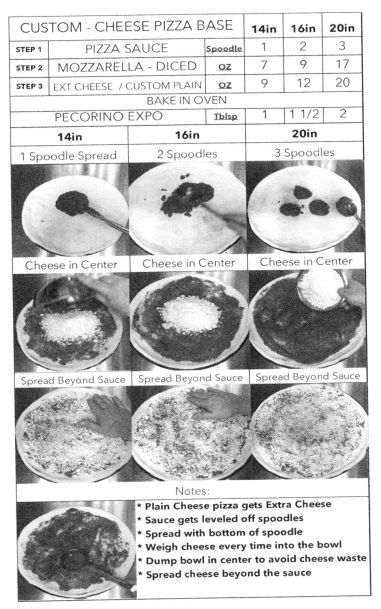

14in	16in	20in
1 Spoodle Spread	2 Spoodles	3 Spoodles
Cheese in Center	Cheese in Center	Cheese in Center
Spread Beyond Sauce	Spread Beyond Sauce	Spread Beyond Sauce

Notes:
* Plain Cheese pizza gets Extra Cheese
* Sauce gets leveled off spoodles
* Spread with bottom of spoodle
* Weigh cheese every time into the bowl
* Dump bowl in center to avoid cheese waste
* Spread cheese beyond the sauce

Pizza recipe card

APPIAN WAY MEATBALLS

STEP 1	MEATBALLS (IN BAKER BOWL)	EACH	3
STEP 2	MARINARA	LADLE	1
STEP 3	MOZZARELLA BALL SLICE TOTAL	SLICES	3
	IN ROTO 3 MINUTES / CONVECTION 3 MIN		
STEP 4	ROMANO GRATED	Tblsp	1/2
STEP 5	SALT PINCH (EXPO)	Pinch	1
	TOGO BOX / SAUCE ON SIDE		LRG

3 MB & MARINARA	MOZZ	3 SLICES

ROMANO	SALT	SERVE

Notes:

Appetizer recipe card

SIGNATURE COCKTAIL VODKA		
STRAWBERRY BASIL LEMONADE		
GLASSWARE	PINT GLASS	
BUILD	SHAKER TIN	
STEP 1	STRAWBERRIES MUDDLED	ITEM	2
STEP 2	BASIL LEAF MUDDLED	ITEM	1
STEP 3	TITOS VODKA	OZ	2
STEP 4	LEMON JUICE	OZ	1.5
STEP 5	SIMPLE SYRUP	OZ	1
ACTION	SHAKE AND STRAIN INTO PINT	
ACTION	TOP SODA	
GARNISH	LEMON WEDGE	

Cocktail recipe card

And you'll need to price out the smartest option for this item. Upon the new menu's release, some items might be removed or sold in less frequency. As a result, the order guide's pars will need to be adjusted for all things affected.

8. KM Trained on It to Train Their Staff

Whoever trains others on how to make these new items properly will require training themselves. This training depends on how long your chain of command is. A meeting with each store's kitchen leader will accomplish this. That assumes they then go on to have their own meeting with their crew. If that is not a possibility, then you need to train the staff. The last thing you want is a new item hitting your menu with a staff that has never heard of it responsible for making it.

9. Revise Menus

Not only the in-house menu but also the to-go menu needs to match what is on the newly created in-house menu *or* menu board.

10. Catering Menu Matches Pricing

This one is on the list because I have made this mistake. I adjusted the in-house pizza prices, only to have a large corporation try to order off an old catering menu online. They were angry, and they expected the prices I had shown online, even though they were the old prices. This mix-up can cause an unnecessary situation. Match it all up.

11. All Menus Sent to Print

Once all menu files are locked, send them to print. Get a reliable ETA for the printed menu so you know you can launch the new menu on the intended launch day.

12. Simultaneous Drop

Monday is a great day to start a new menu. New paper menus ready for Monday means loading the computer menu Sunday night. Do it the night before in case problems arise. Also, change out all paper menus upon Sunday night closing and be sure to dispose of old ones.

13. Online Menu Update

On the day of the release, make sure to update the online menu. That is the PDF on your website, along with any code built into the website. Then find wherever your menu is across review sites and update it there as well.

14. Online Ordering Update

Take the new item's description and pictures and load them into your online ordering menu. Do this the day of the menu release or night before.

15. Third-Party Delivery Update

Ensure any third party you partner with has these updated items and descriptions as well.

16. Food Tastings

A menu launch day can be fun for the staff. If, during the development, some staff got to try the menu items, then great. Day of is excellent for *all* staff to see the correct food item in person and taste it so they can then sell it immediately. Also, staff in the back gets to do trial runs of making the item for someone other than a customer.

17. Marketing in House

Email blast when you believe you have a prepared staff ready to make these new items in a rush. Hopefully, that is day one; if not, wait a week or two to work out the kinks. A release of all these items and their photos on social media should happen in tandem with that.

18. Contact the Press

Make a press release of new menu items and see if you get any local press to pick up the story. Any news segment is good, and you can use the segment clip to re-post online for anyone who doesn't get to see it live.

This system is one of many. Its creation happened over time through trial and error. Here is how I came to create this system. As I mentioned before, when I find a problem, I go to the Basic Leadership Plan of how to solve it. The problem I ran into was that each year I would do some but not all of these steps and items would slip through the cracks. I decided I needed a documented system to avoid failures. So, I followed the steps of a Basic Leadership Plan (BLP):

1. Assess your resources and surroundings.
2. Develop a plan.
3. Communicate effectively.
4. Execute and follow through on the plan.

I assessed the problem. The problem is, I sometimes forget a step when creating a menu and all that goes into it. I developed a plan for a solution; have a list of steps of what a successful menu launch entails. I then communicated that list to myself via saving it on my hard drive, in a place I'd know where to look for it. I saved it with the keywords "Path to a menu." I also communicated the plan as I did it, every time we did it, to my staff. Then I reevaluated that system every time I made a menu item. I performed these steps each time I created a new menu item and looked for edits to the system.

We do new menu items once a year around fall. Some restaurants do it more than that, but you can see that's a lot of info and work to do each time. Sometimes, we'll do a price update if needed, but adding new items works best at one to two times a year. That might sneak up on you at the wrong time unless you plan out a stable part of your year to take this project on. We choose the fall when kids go back to school and before holiday seasons. This choice, like all yearly tasks, should be a part of your calendar planning.

CALENDAR PLANNING

The value of accurate, dependable calendar planning goes beyond meeting planning. You should be planning weekly, monthly, quarterly, semiannual, and yearly events. Anything, from staff birthdays to random annual bills you forget each year. You need to mark that in the calendar, so you prepare for it for next year.

I've had tons of these random "oh shit" moments. The insurance premium for the year is due in February. I'd always forget and boom, it smacks you in the face at the worst possible time. I learned to plan that out. By looking at whatever's coming down the path, I can prepare without surprises. Don't just abide by whatever's on your daily schedule; look at your full year often. Plan out your life and restaurant on a yearly calendar. Look to the next few years as well from time to time.

Schedule out every single task of maintenance. Whether that's calling out a refrigeration tech or planning when to clean it yourself, plan it out. Have it as a calendar update. Have it as an alarm, have it any way that's adhered to dependably. The same thing goes for licensing and marketing. Those should all get prepared this way. Significant events in your community get scheduled in advance. Schedule national holidays and pizza holidays like Pi Day on March 14th, all in advance. Document these on a paper calendar or on a digital calendar you use and share with your team.

Use different colors for different events. Choose any way you want to organize it, but having a calendar and abiding by it is not optional. It's a mandate to have sanity and security that you know what's coming down the pike, and you're ready for it.

IN CONCLUSION

I create systems and tutorials so that there's never a deviation with my staff. The difference between what someone thinks is right vs. what someone knows is right is done with documentation. Instead of the lazy phrase, "Oh, I make this pizza this way," it becomes,

"This is the only right way to make this pizza." Here it is, that's the rule. And if you mess with that or don't do it that exact way, it's fireable. However, if someone says, "Hey, I think it would be better if we made this pizza this way." My response is, "That sounds great. Let's try it." If we decide it's better, we'll change it. We don't go live with it until we perform the path to a menu item protocol. This way, we ensure it is documented and clean before rollout.

If you don't create and maintain systems, you are lazy and don't care about your business. You assume everyone is an idiot because they can't read your mind. But you *do* care, so act like it by creating great systems to kill all the things that annoy you or could be better.

That is the standard. I'm measuring to the standard and creating a system that everyone else has to be accountable to maintain. To stop and think, "What could make this better?" or "What sucks about this?" as we mentioned before, is how you stop, evaluate, and then achieve.

This systematic approach won't make your life harder; it's the opposite. These systems make your life easier. When you invest in the health of your systems, the system maintains the health of your restaurant.

FOR THIS AUDITORY PALATE CLEANSER

Perennial East Bay fixture Rancid's slightly poppier, more hopeful approach by the early 2000s came alive with this song. It's not hard to decipher the meaning of this song. When things go bad, it's nice to have friends there to help prop you back up. Relationships, the economy, reviews, everything that inevitably goes sideways.

Please enjoy,

"Fall Back Down"
by Rancid

CHAPTER 9

HOW TO WIN WITH PEOPLE NOT ON YOUR PAYROLL

W hy would vendors, investors, and even family members want to work with you? You have leverage over your employees because you pay them. When you don't have that power, how do you compel someone to work with you? Sure, you can threaten vendors that you'll pull your business, but working off fear alone does not make for a productive venture. If you are not an amiable, decent person, this road will be a lot harder. Being kind makes life easier. Being inspirational can even make it enjoyable for others.

I'm not saying you should be a nice guy pushover for people to shit on at will. I'm saying if people *want* to work with you, then you will get their best. There will be people who only respond to fear, and those people live in mediocrity. For the people who assume your kindness to be a weakness, you must adjust their view of you. There comes a time when you need to make people keenly aware that you mean business. That you will fuck their world up if they try to take advantage of you. This tactic should never be your first recourse; otherwise, you are the bully. Being an open, thoughtful, and transparent person maintains your integrity. It will also get you where you want to go in this industry when people know they can trust you. Here are the guidelines for nurturing these relationships.

CO-OWNERS

With any co-owners, be it friends or investors, you need to be transparent. Transparency requires you to do these things in advance:

1. Set up each person's title and role.

2. Document everything. Document every situation, every task, and every authority of each member. Avoid excessive overlap. Each task is then vetted to avoid ambiguity and confusion. Ambiguity tears businesses apart.

3. Designate one of you to have "final say." Every member should have oversight on their segment

of the business, but one person must have final say over it all. One person needs to lead, using the input of other owners that they thoughtfully take into account. Each player should have decision-making authority on their primary aspect of the business, as defined by their role, but one person's vision must be able to overrule if needed. That overruling authority should be used sparingly, or there is no team collaboration. As a result, morale will suffer, and those overruled continuously will become apathetic.

4. Define each member's exit strategy. How does one sell their shares or exit without destroying the business? Even if you have no plan to allow for a paid exit, that must be in writing. "Ride or Die" is not a legally binding agreement.

Having co-owners, both Type A who do great in their segment of the business is ideal. This allows you to play to each owner's strengths. Remember, people who are not self-motivated make super shitty owners. People who need constant oversight are employees, not owners. If that's who you have working *with* you, then you need to be their *boss*.

Having the "final say" person maximizing the other owner's gifts is not an owner-boss vs. owner-employee dynamic. It is, rather, a dynamic of teamwork with clear directives. It's not atypical for one person to lead the other co-owner. Mick Jagger leads the business of The Rolling Stones and sets the stage for Keith to be Keith. Mick's studies at the London School for Economics didn't hurt either. Trey Parker runs point for Matt Stone on *South Park*, guiding the show. It can be fortuitous. A co-ownership relationship is most productive when there is clear communication. Achieve this via consistent weekly meetings with clear expectations. There also must be actual repercussions if someone does not get their tasks done on time, and that includes the final say person, who should be leading by example.

Things will not go right all the time. People will have moments of weakness. An owner's bad day can become bad weeks, months, and years if left to rot. When things go south, co-owners must be able to say, "I'm noticing X, Y, and Z—are you?" Do this without emotion or accusation. The person can agree or disagree. Based on the answer, respond, "OK, well, how do you suggest we resolve this?" The key is not getting accusatory or putting the person on the defensive. By asking questions *with* the person, you show the goal is resolution, not accusation. Questions offer a Socratic and non-threatening approach that still gets you to your goal.

Being "right" and "winning" arguments
does not matter in business.

Achieving your mutual goal matters; moving toward a common vision matters. When partners behave like know-it-alls and talk down to other partners, antipathy grows. Then each party loses trust, mutual goals split, and productivity comes to a halt. If this becomes your reality—a non-productive relationship—then who cares if you're right or wrong? Set your sights on the larger goal and choose the most effective way to achieve it. Ego will not get you there. It's all communication. If you know how to communicate with your staff, you can communicate with co-owners, too. You need to remember there's little to no leverage. The only leverage is the shit you have on each other, or you can play the percent ownership game, but again, no one wins there.

Be aware of each owner's direct motivation, including your own. Key into that and make sure your common goals benefit your direct motivations. Getting rich is a typical, popular direct motivator—on paper. In reality, most people who open restaurants go to work each day for something else. If one owner's goal is to make the best pizza possible, then does the environment support that? Are you purchasing the best ingredients and pricing accordingly to make a profit still? If one owner's goal is to create something this town hasn't seen yet, then is the mutual goal to be unique and innovative? If the goal is to cash in, turn and burn on pies, and get out of Dodge, then do both owners strive towards that goal? Communication is the only way to mitigate this and forge ahead cohesively. If everyone does not agree on the vision of success, there will be conflict. This conflict is avoidable if you facilitate a discussion and compromise. If one owner values great reviews, while the other values profit, that can be OK. It's OK as long as all owners agree to work towards all these goals and not treat them like they are mutually exclusive.

Ownership values must be in line, so the shared goal takes precedence over individual pursuits. Conducting business this way means when the shit inevitably hits the fan, you problem-solve together. You're a united front to staff, vendors, and to the problem. For the problem, create an agreed-on BLP to clean up the mess. This way, owners are a team with resolve instead of bickering partners who waste time and resources in the face of adversity.

INVESTORS

Anyone who's investing wants to get their money back. People who invest in a restaurant need to know the nature of the beast. If monetary payments, provisions, and planning aren't clearly mapped out, the partnership can go south. A new restaurant that seems stable can close quickly if their investor gets shaky about first-year sales and the rate of return. I've seen restaurants close because of this exact situation. The owners didn't tell the investors how this industry takes time to build a customer base. Instead, the owners sold them on how rich they'd all get, and when that didn't happen immediately in year one, the investor pulled their money. I've seen investors assume this relationship would mean free dinners and a cushy monthly repayment check. When that didn't happen, because of false pretense, they pulled their money.

I don't like having investors. I prefer working with banks: "You give me this money, and I pay you back under these terms. If X occurs and I cannot pay you back, then I'll be paying this much more at this later date. And if I miss this many payments, then you have the right to do this." If you go with an investor instead, I suggest setting up the relationship as if it were with a bank.

Create a clear, concise contract. What is the investor a part of? Are they a part-owner or just a silent investor? If you have an investor who offers ultimatums more than opinions, you'll have a problem. If your investor says, "I don't like these fancy pizzas, we should stop selling them." Or they say, "I don't like that you don't sell Four Loko, college kids love Four Loko. Sell Four Loko," then you'll have a constant source of trouble and resentment. It will come to a head and be resolved only by establishing agreed-upon boundaries after the fact, or the investor pulling their money.

If investor oversight is a dynamic of your business, then you, the visionary of your business, are answering

to someone else. That means they're in charge and
you do not have the final say. This will be your reality
unless you map out a clear contract defining the terms
of your relationship. Decide in advance what perks, if
any, the investor will receive. Are they allowed to come
in and eat for free, whenever they want, with whom-
ever they bring? Can they do this in profitable as well
as unprofitable months? If you don't say otherwise, why
would they think they can't? You must keep an investor's expectations in check. Learn what the standard
investor relationships are like at your peer restaurants.
Then map out on paper—with a lawyer—the terms of
the relationship you'd be comfortable signing up for.
Only then should you engage and sign with an investor.

BANKS

Bankers, on the other hand, only roll one way. They
only operate with everything locked in on paper. Your
banker won't expect free meals; you can offer if you
want, but it's not going to be a norm. It's super damn
easy to work with a banker. And I am very lucky that our
bank, Security Bank of Tulsa, has always been stand-up
with us. It's a family-run bank. They don't BS, they do
what they say, and we shoot them straight about where
we're at financially. We provide forecasting and tell
them precisely what we see for the fiscal year. We pay
our bills and loans on time, and that's why when we

have a new project, we get money for it with minimal hassle. If you look at a bank as an entity to con, you will screw over only yourself.

If you're thinking that you're the type of person who could never get a bank loan, that is a misconception. Your credit score can get fixed; with clean books, trust, and diligence, you can get funded. I advise using smaller banks, ones who want to see their client's success. If you're any category of a minority or a Veteran, then there are many programs advantageously seeking to get you funded. There are tons of programs out there to make sure you become an American entrepreneur.

If you don't live in America, you'll need to investigate your options so you can also get to where you want to be. If you have shitty credit, fix it. Get your finances in check and build a solid case for how you will make a bank money upon investing in you. Never negotiate based on "why you deserve a loan." No one gives a shit about what you deserve. People and entities only care about what you can do for them.

Side note, I mean no disrespect to the rest of the world. I love France, Italy, Japan. I love these places. I love most people in the places I visit. But there's something about America that's so straight up regarding business. In America, we love going for that brass ring. We, as a culture, respect the concept of anyone achieving anything. That is not the case everywhere else in the world.

FAMILY

Let's talk family. This one is harder. Family can be the greatest blessing a business will ever have. Family can also lead to the shittiest curse a business will ever take on.

The ideal family relationships are like-minded people who cannot break up. Blood relatives cannot divorce you. Ideally, your blood bond outweighs all other relationships. In a perfect scenario, blood relatives get each other on such a deep level that it's like they speak their own language. They share the same background and have like-minded values. They're teammates who have "worked together" for decades, solid before they ever start their business. That's when it's a massive advantage to have a family member working in tandem with you. You fill in their gaps, they fill in yours. Having an unbreakable bond allows for an unmitigated trust that no one can fuck with. That's the ideal.

What's not ideal about family as co-owners is they have a ton of shit on you. Family members have baggage about growing up with you and how you handled your parental relationships. These problems need therapy and time to resolve. Communication is still vital; never assume anything or avoid legal documentation because "it's family." Get an agreement on paper about what is and is not permitted, be it in the restaurant or out of the restaurant. Write down all terms of every situation in advance. Think about things such as, "We will never talk business at home" and/or, "We will never talk personal stuff at work." That can be hard when you live your job all day, every day. You must create boundaries, and all parties must not only agree but actively enforce the agreements.

Beyond other owners as family members, you might have family members as employees. As much as you have monetary leverage over them, things can confuse the issue quickly and turn it into nepotism. Some family business believes the more, the merrier when it comes to family working in their business. Some believe only those that earn their place and drive for it should participate. I lean towards the latter. Tom Cortopassi of Stanislaus Tomatoes is an excellent example of this. The family business of Stanislaus Tomatoes and Corto Olive Oil wasn't handed to Tom. He worked in the business and earned his spot. When the question arose of who should take over, everyone agreed on Tom. That's one of the reasons why that business thrives in the industry today.

Family members are always similar but different. They can find the same things funny and look alike, but their morality and values can be diametrically opposed. People either use their prior pain and life experiences as their resolve or as their excuse. When a family member uses the past to seek excuses instead of solutions, it's a problem. Doing so leads to their life's battles on display in your place of work. The character of resolve means, "No matter what happens, we're going to get it done."

The character of excuse is, "Well, I had this happen to me, so it's not my fault, and it's your problem." This is a very bad situation to be in with business. A family business can tear a family apart. I've seen siblings go years without talking because of their business fallout. Before entertaining the thought of working with a family member, ask this. "Is their character rooted in excuses, or are they rooted in resolve?"

You can write down on paper, "We will not let this break up our family," but there's nothing guaranteeing it will stick. You need to have a heart-to-heart with yourself when you get into business with a family member. Ask yourself, "Am I OK losing this member of my family as a result of this business?" There's a very real possibility that you will. For certain, you will never look at that person the same way again, in some positive or negative ways. It's possible to develop a disdain for them. Is that something you are OK with?

To mitigate this, analyze everything you don't like about that person first and then address it. You need to examine their dependability above all else. Will this person die for you? Would you die for them? If not, it's not worth doing business with them; it won't work.

Heed this advice now:

If your family member, the one you are about to become partners with, would not die for you, do not go into business with them.

VENDORS

For vendors and everyone that you're ever going to work with, here are some basic rules to follow. Be open, be honest, be transparent. Case in point, you have one food vendor, they're excellent on price, but their prices start to creep up. Another food vendor comes to your restaurant and says, "Hey, you know I could beat that flour price. I saw your invoice, and I can save you some money." The wrong thing to do is to switch business right then and there and buy from the new vendor without informing your current vendor. Don't then wait until the original supplier brings it up and say, "Well, hey, you were screwing me on price, so I had to switch." That's bad business. That does not build trust.

The ethical decision at that moment would be to give the first vendor the right of first refusal. You should say, "Hey, this other company is coming in and trying to steal your thunder. They're reading my invoices, which I'm not too stoked about. Nonetheless, they can give me a better price. Now, if it were just a few cents difference, I'd let it go, but it's a massive difference in price. What can you do here?" And then leave it to them.

If they're truly a team player, they will do what they can, be open about their pricing, and work to get you to where you need to be. If they're a shitty salesperson, they'll haggle you on something else to make their quota and disregard your concern. You must disengage from people like this and say, "Since we're not even in the ballpark on price, I need to switch vendors on that item. I'm sure you understand." That is how you sleep at night and also get to your goal.

For negotiating prices, I understand not being a completely open book. At some point, you need to say, "Here's why I would switch. Tell me why I shouldn't." If the argument you hear makes sense, agree, and don't switch. If it is BS, call it out and be transparent why you aren't going with them on this item.

The Best Negotiating Question You Can Ask

"Is that really the best price you can give me?" Really pour it on when you ask, like you don't believe the price can be what it is. The beauty of that question is, it's very direct, "Is this *really* the best price?" Because either they'll say yes, and assuming you trust them, you'll know you're getting their best price. If they're lying, you'll eventually find out and you'll fire them as a vendor. That is assuming that they didn't know that it wasn't the best price either. When a new person comes along who wants to steal the current vendor's thunder, again, always give right of first refusal to existing vendors. Be loyal. There is a value to that in this industry. Shifty vendors will short bid items to try and get a foot in the door. They'll then slowly creep prices up if you don't pay attention. I advise choosing the devil you know first before assuming the grass to be greener on the other side of the fence.

Side note: Keep a spreadsheet of your costs per item, per store, that you update with every invoice. If you are checking numbers like a hawk, it will be a lot harder to pull a fast one over on you. Inputting invoices takes a few hours a week to save thousands a year.

Another thing about dealing with vendors is to ask them about their lives. They are people, too. You don't need to follow their social media feed and go to their soccer games, but you can have a drink or coffee with them now and then. Know them on a personal level. That's good business. They're part of your business life. So, make your life more agreeable and be kind to them, but make it very, very clear to never confuse your kindness for weakness. Offer them a slice of pizza or a full pizza to take home to their family, but if they take one without you giving consent, delete the relationship. Never let yourself get taken advantage of. If you do see yourself getting taken advantage of, provide them with one get out of jail free card, announce what you will not tolerate. Then if they get a second strike, sever the relationship. At that point, you are severing the relationship with complete integrity. You didn't ghost them; you moved your business away from a vendor who doesn't value you.

These practices pertain to face-to-face vendors. For all online or phone relationship vendors, there is another set of standards. For all companies you do business with, demand a direct rep for your company. Your ISP, credit card processor, no matter how far away or how small a business, require they provide you a rep. For any business you give money to, you have the right to a single representative to run issues through. If they say, "We can't give you a rep," then you should say, "Well, the other company will, so I'm going to do business with them."

Reps can cost money for the vendor, but you need to have a direct line of communication for all things you give money to. Otherwise, you'll be on the phone with tech support for ten hours every other Wednesday. Having reps saves you time and keeps your mental effort for what you need to be doing, working on your business. Some companies you *need* to work with won't have reps. For these, delegate someone on your team to handle them, so it doesn't monopolize your time.

Getting Harsh with Vendors

I aspire to be a nice guy. I try to do right by people. I sleep well at night because I don't screw people over. Sometimes, you need to be an asshole. Not an overt asshole, but a temporary asshole for the sake of your business. You need to get harsh with a vendor. You correct their perception and say, "Oh, you were under the impression that I would roll over for your bullshit. No, motherfucker, don't fuck with me or I will invite pain into your life." Because sometimes people won't understand until you get to that level. Sometimes, you need to be domineering. Young or old, guy or girl, big or small, strong, fat, thin, *it doesn't matter.* It's all about presence.

In the Marine Corps, the guy I was most scared of was 5 ft. 4in. When he looked at me in my eyes, I knew he meant business. Like he could kill you three times before you hit the floor. Even if I could beat him up, I would never even think to do so because he carried himself in a way that projected strength. That's the look in your eyes you need to have when you're being fucked with.

Getting harsh and lighting up a vendor is not appropriate the first time your pizza box price rises by eight cents. Getting harsh is appropriate when you are clearly getting taken advantage of. Get harsh when someone you need to work with or deal with is not responding. Sometimes, this needs to occur with vendors, sometimes, with government authorities or institutions. Show respect, speak tactfully, and speak truths, not opinions. Also, avoid the F-bomb curses you want to say. Cursing in a heated conversation with a vendor you aren't close with means you lost. It shows you lost your cool and are not in control. Curse when you know this is a group or person that you know already commonly curses. Sometimes, a well-placed expletive can work, but it should never be directed at someone.

A good example with a vendor you know: "I need to know what the fuck we're doing here, guys."

A bad example: "And if you don't get it right, you can go fuck yourself."

The bad example is an attack. Attacks don't lead to progress.

The first time I got harsh with a vendor was two months after opening my first store. Coke wouldn't give me bag in a box system (BIB); I received kegs of Coke instead. They thought freshness would be an issue with a restaurant so small. That puts into perspective how little people believed in us. Even Coca-Cola didn't want to chance selling us a BIB, assuming we'd never sell it all before hitting the expiration of the product. I was selling a pile of kegs a week and the rep wasn't smart enough to take notice on their own. I told him, "I need a BIB system asap, I don't have the space to keep all these Coke kegs."

I kept getting, "Oh, we'll do that next week." Then it became, "We think we'll get you a new system next month." I kept getting the runaround of we'll do this, we'll do that. This was a bad rep, no disrespect to Coke. I love Coca-Cola and work with them to this day. They had a shitty person working for them, as we all have had, and I was too green to know someone else to reach out to.

Not knowing my options, but knowing I was getting fucked with, I did the following. I rounded up all the kegs, drove to the Coke facility they came from, and said, "Here are all your kegs back. The next thing I'm bringing is your fountain system after I rip it out unless

I get a proper BIB system. Or I'll just sell beer 'til I get a Pepsi system installed." The dock worker I dropped the kegs off to got a hold of the sales team leader—the boss of my rep at the time.

I got an apology from Coke, and boom, I had a BIB system the next day.

When shit goes sideways, be direct, clear, and emphatic about your point. Get things done face to face when possible; it moves the needle quicker. In this situation I didn't curse, didn't yell, and still made my point and accomplished my goal.

Next Level Vendor Relationships

For local vendors who do great work, i.e., photographer, sign companies, or print shops, help them win with you. Post a photo of you using their service on social media and endorse them publicly. By you vouching for them, they get more business; you become an invaluable customer.

When you manifest your influence to mutually benefit you and the people that do great work for you, both parties win. They get more business, *and* they value your relationship above others. They'll seek to improve their relationship with you at all times and treat you like a VIP.

Even a basic service repair that requires a technician to come out to fix, I want to make that interaction a win. When a refrigeration unit needs repair, and they send a new tech, I make sure that tech gets treated with dignity and respect in our restaurant. When they're done working, we'll give them a slice of pizza and a soda or water for free. This is the protocol for all our managers to practice. That way, when there's an after-hours emergency, and we're among many businesses calling with an issue, they'll want to choose us first. Because we're friendly, we pay on time, and they're getting a free meal out of it. At the same time, we're back up and running that much quicker. Good leads to good.

Using the term "win-win" sounds super cliché, corporate, and lame. But making life suck less for the people around you makes people want to be around you and your business. We use a third-party food delivery service. We get different delivery people coming in all night. By treating them with respect, looking them in the eye, and saying thank you, they will want to deliver for us. They want to choose yes when our store pops up on their app, as opposed to the restaurants that treat them like human garage when they walk in. No person is garbage ...well, some are, but I try to think that most people aren't, or at least anyone that would come into contact with my business isn't.

The goal is to leave all people who interact with our restaurant with a positive impression. Not just our customers. The impressive experience goes beyond who we sell to. I need anyone who comes into Andolini's to say, "That was a solid restaurant run by solid people, and I dig what they do." If our actions don't support that conclusion, we need to unfuck ourselves.

Ask Strategy

Did you even try to ask? The worst that can happen is someone says no. You've heard that before, but it's true. So often, the fear of rejection stops us from saying what's on our mind: "Hey, can I get a better deal on that?" It's just like we mentioned before, "Is that *really* the best price possible?" Those are two very honest ways to negotiate. I call it Ask Strategy. Do you want something cheaper? How about, "Can I get a custom logo version of that item?" or, "What can I do to get that custom item at a discounted rate?" Even if it is a great price, when you ask if something could be better, you find out you're sometimes right. Ask Strategy gets this done.

When I was a little kid growing up in New Jersey, I took karate. I was a dorky kid, but I was very deserving of a yellow belt. That's not the adult version of me inflaming the ego of nine-year-old me. I really did deserve it. I worked a lot harder than the other kids in the class, and I thrived off the discipline. Having a Marine Lieutenant Colonel father had prepared me well for this. The teacher—or Sensei—wanted to do promotions for all the kids who came in at the same time, even though I was well ahead of them. My parents said, "We're going to tell him he needs to give you a higher belt now. You haven't missed a class, and you deserve it." I said, "No, I don't want that." Even at nine years old, I didn't want help. Then they said, "Well then, you need to say to him that you deserve a better belt and to go ask for it." Again, me wanting the higher belt to be a pure win, I wanted no interference. Wanting to earn it purely is nice, clean, and noble.

It's not what business is or how business works.

If you want something better, you go out and ask for it. If you don't get the result you wanted, keep asking and maneuvering until you do. Keep pushing, keep taking, because the takers fuel their vision, and the people who wait are left waiting forever indignantly.

Fast forward to my high school self, now living in the Bay Area of California. Again, these are dated references to awkward teen years, but they do relate. I loved hearing the school announcements each day. I loved them because, during my freshman year, I listened to a senior who was fantastically sarcastic perform them, and I wanted his job. Both sophomore and junior year, I tried out for the announcements and didn't get it. It was given to a senior each year. Then, when it was my senior year—my year to do it—they had no tryouts. I was at a loss. I had been waiting three years to get this job to make stupid jokes for all my friends to hear, and no dice. I listened to the president of the AV club do the announcements day one of my senior year, with no tryout mentioned.

I could have sulked, called BS, and left it at that. Instead, I went to the "nerdium" that is the De La Salle High School AV Room, and asked, "What's going on with tryouts this year?" They said, "Well, we already have a crew, so we're set." I then said, "Well, I really would like to do it. Do you have a problem if I do the announcements?" They replied, "There's no need. We already have this locked up." I said, "If you think someone can do this better than me, choose *them*; you know I'm serious about this, I've tried out the last two years, and I want to do this. Do you have any issue with me doing this?" They said, "No, not really, one less thing for us to worry about." There you go. The thing I had waited for three years I got because I asked. Instead of throwing a hissy fit or saying the world screwed me over and being angry, I asked and got my way. Sometimes, that's all it takes. I'm not unique or extremely talented. I am headstrong, though, and willing to put myself out there. I also learned from this that when I wanted something and went after it, it was a lot easier than waiting for the world to give it to me.

The world does not care about you enough to have a plan to give you things.

When we opened Andolini's, I wanted to have our logo on our pizza box. I hated bland, mass-produced boxes. I knew we'd never get brand recognition that way.

Pizza box vendors would say to us, "You're too small to have it. You don't do nearly enough volume." Instead of me saying, "Well, OK, fine. I guess that's that." I said, "What do you need from me for me to have a pizza box that has our logo on it?" They said, "If you use one printing plate for all your sizes and guarantee that you will buy one thousand cases, then we can do it." I got my logo on a box as a brand-new single store location. This meant our fourteen-inch box design was also a fourteen-inch design on our twenty-inch box, but I found a solution. I found a workaround, and I got the goal met.

Everything that you want is doable by asking. When you get a "no," find a workaround to the ask and move until you get what you need. Ask fair, ask righteous, ask in a friendly manner, ask with pure intentions, but always ask. To have your ask heard, frame it as a win for both parties. For example, "I want to sell more pizza, and if I have this rare item on the menu, it helps me stand out. That means more customers for *me*, and me buying more product from *you*. What do you need from me to be able to stock this item?"

I can accept a *no* if the reason I can't have what I ask for is just and makes sense. But that is a rare occurrence. To people who don't have what they want, they most likely didn't put in the work to get it. If the goal is only to ask once, you will fail. If the goal is to ask enough times in enough ways until your goal is achieved, you will achieve your goal.

This industry isn't built on the backs of people who gave up. It's about plugging away until your mental reality is actual reality. If an idea in your head annoys you that it's not real, then plan it out and make it real. Ask every person whose help you will need to achieve it. They can only say no. When they do say no, build your workaround.

GOVERNMENTAL ORGANIZATIONS YOU ANSWER TO

If you don't have a seat at the table, you're on the menu. Years of dealing with the health department had frustrated me. I pride myself on running an immaculate restaurant. Our local health department would go after really obscure rules and bypass important ones. I would get annoyed to see another restaurant with their vegetables on the ground, outside their loading dock not getting shut down. Meanwhile, we are getting dinged for a server with barely shoulder-length hair not in a ponytail. I would hear nightmare stories from other Tulsa restaurants, and, for a long time, it was common to complain and bitch about the Tulsa Health Department.

I'd hear stories about the rules changing from store to store. Some restaurants had issues with different agents having conflicting agendas on how to interpret certain rules. After twelve years of that, I got annoyed and asked myself, "Why am I doing nothing about this?" This ambiguity was genuinely wrong, and it's not in the public health's best interest. The health department needs to be concerned with temperature controls and things that keep the customer safe. Instead, they were acting like California Highway Patrol officers measuring the distance of a parked car from the curb. The kind of official who gives a fine to someone who doesn't say hi to them the right way, or so was the perception.

I set up a meeting with the head of the health department, who took my meeting immediately upon request. He said he wanted more feedback from restaurant owners and could only talk to his subordinates if he had something to go off of. I pointed out the good things I had noticed, and then I pointed out the litany of bad. He was mortified and asked me, "Why did you abide by their dictates when they made outlandish conflicting requests?" I responded, "I didn't know I had an option not to." He said, "Well, you could always talk to me because that is not what I want our health department officials doing." As a result, we came to a consensus. A few health department officials were fired, and the rest were retrained.

The problems and mission of that local agency shifted to become more productive. Now our relationship with the health department isn't only amicable, it's positive. I had a similar situation with the Alcohol Beverage Law Enforcement (ABLE) commission in Oklahoma. They had processed our annual check for a license at one of our locations, which made us believe that that license was active. In fact, they had lost the signed application—so the license wasn't active—and because of their antiquated system, we were out of compliance. Months went by with me calling in every month, asking for our physical license, only to be told, "Yep, it's in the mail. We can see it processed."

Then one day out of nowhere, with customers in our restaurant, armed ABLE police go in and shut down one of my locations for not having a license. Let me stop here and explain. I am not bullshitting this story. This is verbatim what occurred. ABLE and I both have documented it. I'm not fudging facts; we were shut down for ninety minutes though we had a paid license for that location and while holding seven other active alcohol licenses fully in compliance with no citations. ABLE police officers, an Oklahoma entity created decades ago to stop bootleggers, then threatened my staff and my managers with fines. According to ABLE, they *personally* were also in violation of not having an active license on premise and could be fined. Additionally, this suburban location, comprised of the most straight-laced employees I have, could be fined, and our restaurant shut down.

I raised holy hell with the officers on the phone, never cussing, but explaining the lunacy. They didn't believe the home office could make such an egregious error. But the home office definitely had done exactly that. I called their offices and every government entity I could get ahold of. After forty-five minutes, they realized that they had cashed a check...only because I had the proof *they* didn't have. The administrative arm and enforcement arms of ABLE weren't communicating well...but they finally called off their police officers. My staff and I received an emphatic apology from every officer there and the director of ABLE. Further, ABLE changed their protocol for how they process applications. They also changed how they adjudicate out-of-date licenses, so a mistake like this would never happen again.

This change was accomplished by meeting with ABLE to talk about how to redo their system. I should've done this years earlier. If you're not fixing the problem, you're bound to be a victim of it, or worse, part of the problem. I decided I need to be on every board and group that allows private business owners to make decisions related to restaurants. I'm not seeking to be a politician, but I'm sure as shit also not looking to be messed with. When I get involved, I avoid a problem for me and other like-minded businesses. The power to create change can occur by merely attending a meeting once every few months. If nothing else, I know who I need to know for potential problems and can expand my network of influence.

A network of influence also leads to more pizzas sold. So for all the things that are annoying you, whatever governmental problems that piss you off, there is a workaround. You can talk to them or their boss or their boss's boss. And when no one wants to help resolve it, make a strong case, and then show your intent to talk to the press. Because that's your right, and usually that'll lock and load someone pretty damn quick to help you out for fear of bad PR. I don't threaten to go to the press or legal action as my first maneuver, but it's undoubtedly in my toolbox.

This notion that the little guys always get pushed around and have no recourse is bullshit, especially in the age of social media. You have a following; you have a platform. Push back or, better yet, work with agencies that don't understand your world to incite change.

OTHER RESTAURANTEURS

At Las Vegas Pizza Expo 2019, I stopped to reflect on the industry of Pizza Makers. I saw all walks of the industry working together and learning from one another, and this stayed with me. I realized the concept of having enemies is a very old-fashioned notion. Working with your competition is significantly smarter than having enemies. Genuinely working with your competition has way more benefits than an antagonistic relationship. Whether it's locally or nationally, knowing people in this industry and being on the same page about pushing it forward is a smart move.

Locally, you might not want another pizza place to open up across the street from you, and I get that. No one wants to split their market share. However, having businesses that fill in the gaps for one another and create a "scene" or "district" is a win for your business. You want your location to be part of a "scene." That's the way you move the needle. If you disagree, open in the middle of a desert and see how much business you get with the absence of competition. Being in touch with your competition means that when you have an issue, you have a resource. A resource for licensing issues, or bouncing ideas off of, you have someone else in the game with you. You can discuss market strategies, tech tips, and have a friend not on your payroll. These are all reasons to make nice with your competition.

Another plus to having a good relationship with other local owners is sharing a talent pool. When you have to fire someone you don't want to fire, they can now hire them and vice versa. This increases your talent pool. I've been in this position multiple times. I had to let someone go because they did something that was just stupid enough I had to. I didn't want to let them go, but it wouldn't be living to the standard if I did not fire them. I want people in these situations to still land on their feet. A good relationship with another restaurant owner allows me that opportunity.

Upon my arrival at Marine Corps OCS, they gave us one book to read on our own, not as part of the curriculum. It was Sun Tzu's *The Art of War*. That's a pretty hardcore book to be given on day one with no context.

In it, it says, "Know thy enemy, and know thyself." I think we could take the word enemy and modify it to competition, and it makes more sense for today. After all, we're not at war; this is cheese on bread we're talking about. Know thy competition means to know what they're going for. Know what you're going for as well. Our goal is not to destroy the competition but rather to complement them and fill in the gaps their brand leaves behind. This way, both businesses thrive, survive, and succeed. If other businesses on your street are closing, that's not good for you. A closing hurts your district's customer perception and the viability of your location's market value.

Don't get angry at the competition and blame them for your business problems. That's misplaced hostility. Appropriately deal with that by exercising or get therapy. Hating on other restaurants will not make your restaurant more successful.

This is a 100% absolute fact; you will never be more successful because of the negativity you spread about other restaurants. The only way to win is by being the best you can be, always learning, and letting go of unproductive bullshit.

IN SUMMARY

If you treat people with respect, genuine respect, you gain respect in turn. When you find ways for those in your circle of influence to win with you, it fuels growth. You can attempt to dominate every relationship, but that will build resentment and lead to more obstacles in your path.

FOR THIS AUDITORY PALATE CLEANSER

David Letterman would regard them as the only band dedicated to the "Fight of Foo." Letterman also touted them as his favorite band. For me, this song is about the journey and the chase for relevance. When one thing gets done, it's time for the next thing. I try to remind myself to stop and enjoy it, but life, like this song, keeps building and pounding, never relenting with twists and turns, a lot like this job.

Please enjoy,

"All My Life"
by Foo Fighters

CHAPTER 10

SO, YOU'RE THE SHIT NOW?

HOW TO GET GREAT REVIEWS AND AWARDS TO DOMINATE YOUR MARKETING

What is marketing anymore? What was marketing to begin with? Spend money to make money, right? If I invest in my business to tell more people about it, so they come in, then that's marketing, right? That's the theory behind it, but what about spending money because you're supposed to spend it? The preconceived notion of doing what has already been done is more antiquated than ever. You don't need to spend money just because that's what people do. Your biggest marketing weapon is you, your face, your ingenuity, and your effort, and it's time you use it.

My wife is a real estate agent in Tulsa. She is very successful at what she does. When she started as an agent, she got pressured to buy marketing ads in local magazines. The ones you read at the doctor's office. If you read those magazines, you'll see there are a lot of realtors spending money to place an ad about their current properties. Common thought would be, "If these other successful realtors are doing this, then I should, too." My wife has watched my marketing for years. We talked about what works and what doesn't. She knew this wasn't a good spend of investment dollars.

Realtors get advice to spend a certain percentage of their sales each month on marketing. So that becomes the goal, to spend money. These magazines know that and seek realtors as easy money. Thousands of dollars a month, to show a glamor shot photo of them with a property that hasn't been on the market in weeks. What's the win? Where's the ROI? But like sheep to the slaughter, they have a long line of realtor ad spend each month. Who goes to a magazine to find a realtor anymore? Most people ask a friend or go online. So why do they still do it? Realtors do it because that's what they assume they're supposed to be doing because they saw someone else do it.

My wife realized this and made a free Yelp profile. Out of the five thousand active agents in Tulsa, there were only six who had claimed a Yelp page and only four who loaded their pictures. My wife got lead after lead, which turned into multiple sales. Many were out-of-towners who typed "Tulsa Real Estate Agent" into Google. Yelp search engine optimization (SEO) works to put Yelp results at the top when a relevant phrase is typed. Mind you, this isn't paid Yelp ads we're talking about, this is loading a profile in five minutes and walking away.

Claiming your Yelp page is not an in-depth, high-level marketing plan that took time to develop. This is avoiding stupidity, which is a lot of what marketing is today. New operators will get inundated with sales calls and emails about all the promotional products they should buy. They'll get sales calls about the ad space in posters at the local school you should buy to show your support. It is shit piled on top of shit that benefits no one except the out of state poster company.

MARKET MODERNLY

A lot of pizzerias do the same thing as the realtors who paid for local magazine ads. They do what they've seen done before. I know some old school pizzerias that still do door hangers and put ads in the *Penny Saver* and Valpak. Why? Because that's what you do, right? I'm not saying door hangers won't work at all. For a small percentage of the population, you will get a return, with a horrible ROI. If you want a younger demo, which you do, then savvy social media marketing is king. Additionally, the choices eighteen- to forty-five-year-olds make influence the forty-five- to-sixty-five-year-old demo. That's why this demo is perpetually sought after.

If you're reading this fifty years after I wrote it, then I don't know what's cool for you in your day and age. I don't know what hologram-based robot space marketing the kids are into. I do know there'll be something; for a fact, there will be a new method of delivery. Currently, it's social media. Social media was free for about a decade. Then it stopped being 100% free, and in the year 2020, when I'm writing this, Instagram is the new hotness. That is currently free-ish, but steadily getting more monetized.

Here is the macro message: choose affordable, direct ways that target your customer. The more effort you put into personalizing your message to that customer, the better. People will never tire of people showing an interest in them. People will never grow tired of feeling special. Whatever marketing does that, run toward it. Cookie-cutter bland media approaches are dead. Dead forever.

Marketing is now based upon engagement. It's based upon your customers' engagement in your brand's story, so you connect to their story. Salesmanship now is endearing yourself to the customer. A stock image of a pizza with a bland slogan does not accomplish this. Solid marketing is building a connection and channeling an emotional response—a sense of longing or wanting to be a part of something.

Of course, you want to monetize the customer's hunger. Great food photos and intriguing specials accomplish this. But can you get a non-hungry customer to crave the way you, your restaurant, your pizza, and your brand make them feel? Do they feel happy thinking about having a drink at your bar with your staff? Do they long to open your pizza box at their home while they watch their favorite team? Do they think fondly of enjoying their free time with their family at a table in your restaurant? These are the emotional pulls you need to evoke to generate repeat business. I am describing the same individual's emotional responses, getting tapped in three different ways, via bar sales, take-out, and dine-in.

Endearing yourself to the customer isn't new, but it's never been more critical than it is today. Thirty-five years ago, the pulse of pizza marketing was the speed of service. In the '90s, it was kookie pizzas and letting everyone know your location. It wasn't that easy in the '90s to let people know you existed. The phone book was the way you announced your existence pre-Internet. The 2000s were more history-driven marketing, such as, "Look at what my great-grandparents taught me when they came from the old country." The 2010s became more science-based, touting the ingredient mix and sourcing you used.

Now it's, "What up world? It's your boy hanging out, making the dough. Check this out." In other words, it's story-based marketing. What's your story? What do you stand for? Where and why does your brand exist, and why should I care? This gets conveyed via videos. Videos shot in selfie mode with little to no camera operating skills, and yet somehow it resonates. The only constant is change. Selfie mode videos will, at some point, become passé. Currently, in the 2020s, it's the personal reality era; that's where marketing thrives. Whatever way you get your message out, choose what is personal, builds interest, and endears yourself to the customer.

TAKE A LESSON FROM UFC, WWE FOR PERSONA BUILDING

There's an interesting dynamic in the UFC for what matches get the most Pay Per View sales. The two top champion fighters will not get as many buy-ins as two fighters that openly hate each other. A fight based on a grudge match makes more money. Why is that? Why are lesser fighters getting more intrigue? It's because there's a story. It's because you can get emotionally invested in their conflict.

Another example is the marketing juggernaut of World Wrestling Entertainment, formerly WWF. WWE takes two characters...and yes, I'm aware it's scripted... and they create an emotional pull. The winner is mapped out ahead of time, but they give the viewer a sports opera with a climactic crescendo. They act out a fight and weave a story as rich as any *Rocky* film, also scripted and also awesome. I started watching wrestling a few years back for the first time since the '90s and saw genius marketing. Just astounding how well they capitalize on their audience. There is a lot to learn from WWE if you can get over your preconceived notions of wrestling being hokey.

WWE goes in month-long spurts building a story, leading to a Pay-Per-View where they then cash in on that build. They'll pull real-life backstory about the wrestlers to create conflict. It's an athletic theatre that creates drama to build intrigue. Additionally, their real-life work ethic is right on par with what it takes to be a successful restaurant owner. They have a nonstop fifty-two-weeks-a-year schedule that relies on in-house ticket sales, concessions, and social media. It's a colossal undertaking run by a family, the McMahons. Not too dissimilar from your typical pizzeria owner who works with family and never takes a day off.

In wrestling, there is the bad guy, or "heel," whose job is to get you to hate them loudly. There's the good guy, or "babyface," who will perform a hero's journey to win the good fight. It's an emotional ploy that elicits a reaction. The braggy "heel" or "face" story is as old as storytelling itself. The goal is to get people to cheer *or* boo; because as long as they care, that's the win.

As an adult, I can recognize "heel" or bad-guy tactics used famously by celebrities for attention—celebrities who are outside of wrestling who were influenced by it and use it for their own personal gain.

Famous music producer Rick Rubin played a heel in the '80s. Type "Rick Rubin, Beastie Boys" into Google.

You'll see Rick gloating to the camera about how no one was ever going to be better than the Beastie Boys. That when they finally made a music video for MTV, they were going to have to rename MTV to "Beastie TV." He said it with such braggadocio confidence it built intrigue. The Rick Rubin of today is a very mild, chill, meditative guy. A famously successful producer, with a long beard living peacefully in Malibu. How did that guy become this guy? Well, it's because he was never that guy to begin with. Rick was a wrestling fan. He imitated Rick Flair, the show-stopping, styling, pro-filing wrestler of the 1970s. That braggart spirit lends itself to sales. Every rapper for the last forty years falls into the same category, and it works. Conor McGregor, Floyd Mayweather, Muhammad Ali, all have said they imitated "heel" wrestlers. All of them got rich off using it to pour gas on the fire of their careers.

Not all wrestling characters are braggarts. Some are the endearing underdog. Some are the old warhorse look-ing for their final shot. Some are the overconfident young buck about to make a name for themselves. All of them build intrigue; all of them have a story that pulls you in. That begs the question, what is *your* story, and why should I care? Answer that with a compelling hook, and you have now marketed yourself and your business to me.

I am the face of my company. When in public, I am myself, but the on-stage version of myself. My on-stage version isn't introverted and quiet like I am at home. I am outward and overly gregarious to those around me. I know some owners whose persona is the angry braggart yelling at the camera. They create a mix between a used car salesman and Gordon Ramsey. This is playing the "heel" version of themselves, and I have seen it work. I've seen restaurants trash talk about their competition and even their customers, and it worked. It's not for me, but it is possible to pull off if done tongue in cheek. Bear in mind, many of the most popular wrestlers started as heels. The Rock, Stone Cold, Ric Flair all gained popularity as bad guys. People love a compelling bad guy. I don't advise it, but it is possible.

If being the face of your company is hard for you, I highly suggest you work through that. Map out your on-stage persona so you can say, "I'm not me. I'm the persona." I'm not saying be fake or not genuine. I'm saying to play your role well might mean being a little over the top. To speak outwardly about myself or my business is inherently awkward for me. In that regard, this whole book is awkward for me. But when I act like someone who's an advocate for my business, like Paul Heyman is in WWE for his wrestler clients, I get my message across. (Google Paul Heyman promo to see a level of showmanship and oratory ability unrivaled.)

This is the sizzle to the steak. You still have to have a damn good steak, but it sure as shit doesn't hurt to have some sizzle along with it. This is how you sell it. This is how you market. This is how you become the face and spokesperson for your brand. A spokesperson is an expensive thing, but you aren't. You're already there, and by being the person with the mic, you just gave a face, a story, and a reason to go to your pizzeria. This is an advantage none of the big chains have.

MAXIMIZE YOUR BRANDING AND PACKAGING

"Sell me this pen" is a sales drill predicated upon selling an item of little to no significance, value, or individuality. It takes the salesmanship of the individual seller to sell it to someone. Dollar-store pens aren't a particularly exciting item from a brand perspective. People don't use the pen purchase as an expression of their personality, at least not yet. A better brand sales example is bottled water. Water, one of the most abundant resources in the world, is sold in bottled form in a multitude of ways at an incredible markup. What does your bottled water say about you? There's the big box warehouse club, thin plastic bottle, bottled water. What about the clean lines and sleek design of the electrolyte-enhanced bottled water? The significant beverage players of Pepsi and Coca Cola have Aquafina and Dasani. All selling an identical product with different packaging. How and why do we care?

I love packaging. I fucking love it. I love the ability packaging has to elicit a response. I've loved packaging all my life, which is a very odd statement. My brother mocked me as a kid for how much I loved packaging. I wanted Lunchables but only got deli meat and crackers in a baggie from my mom. As a dumbass kid, I didn't realize the deli meats in the baggy were a higher quality than what was in the clean yellow Lunchables box. The packaging had me. It still does. I love the perfect lines of an unopened Apple product or the sleek design of a well-packaged item of clothing. Packaging is marketing.

Does someone have a preference for their water, really? Can someone tell the difference between these waters in a blind taste test? With that said, people choose their bottled water because it represents them in some way. Even the self-fill eco-aware Nalgene bottle is still a brand purchase. It demonstrates their value system via how they hold their water. For all the non-reusable purchasers, the millions of them, they all choose a brand to represent them. Even the ones who choose cheap water, *choose* the cheap version and spend good money on it.

I was at a very nice restaurant in Miami, Bazaar by Jose Andres. They brought water to the table—again, this is water—and it was in a bottle of Alexander Wang Evian. This is a high-end couture fashion designer who made a bottle of water, and now it's an upsell on the bill. Here's the lesson I got from all this:

Yes, the actual flavor and quality of your pizza does matter. But don't underestimate the power of salesmanship and monetizing your brand. A solid brand placement can take a nothing pizza and make it into a something pizza. An award-worthy pizza might never receive any recognition if the ambiance and packaging of that pizza experience is generic. The brand can take the same generic widget and make it classy, luxurious, and in-demand. Also, it can accomplish the inverse and say hey, I'm cheap and affordable, buy me. Two different bottles with different logos, the same content, perceived differently. That perception creates the ability to charge less or more.

In the pizza industry, having a great product, with a great brand that builds positive perception, leads to increased profitability. It is incredibly difficult to compete with turn-and-burn "cheap" pizza. The choice is either selling based on convenience or experience. You are not everywhere and can't make money on cheap or convenience. You can win on providing an experience. You can win on being endearing. You can win when you find channels to speak directly to the customer. In turn, your customers will feel great for knowing they chose the best and that you are that choice. That's the essence of how you market great food via messaging, branding, and execution.

KNOW YOUR "CLEAN SLATE" MARKETING PLAN

What should your marketing plan be? Here is the answer to that broad question with a simple solution. If not one customer came in today, what would you do? For whatever reason, no one will walk in your doors today. You have no orders; you have nothing. Not one dollar will hit your register unless you make a move. What is *that* move?

That move is now your marketing plan. If no one was going to come in today, I would go out, and I would do X, Y, Z. There you go, X, Y, Z is now your new marketing plan. Try X, Y, Z, see what the return on investment is, and then assess if you should choose to modify it, build on it, or ditch it. That's your marketing plan.

Way too often, businesses rely on their existing base instead of farming new sales. A marketing strategy is going after new customers as much as it is tending to existing ones. Existing customers move on for various reasons. You *must* have a customer acquisition strategy at the forefront of your marketing plan. Existing customer marketing gets nurtured by a consistently impressive dining experience. Loyalty programs can help cater to existing customers. Don't allow a loyalty program to train the customer only to come when an award is on the line. Otherwise, your value proposition will become rooted in the incentivization of the customer and nothing else. Instead, market to attain customers who want to keep coming back because of the food and not because of the discount.

In 2008, I needed new customers badly. What we were doing wasn't enough. This was the first time I asked myself the clean slate question. What would I do to get a whole new set of customers ASAP? We were on the brink of closing. Several new restaurants opened—many of them buffets—and it was killing my lunch business. I had the white-collar income on the weekends, but that wasn't enough revenue to carry the restaurant. The blue-collar lunch crews were what I needed. I wasn't about to put in a buffet; I didn't have the space, equipment, or inclination to become a buffet. So I created an unlimited combo of as much pizza, salad, and pasta as you want. Just keep ordering and we'll keep bringing it to you. That gave me my lunch crowd. That helped make me a contender against the buffets.

Another time we needed to come up with a way to gain new customers, I believed if I spoke in a heartfelt way about my business and gave people a discount to *try* us, we would get traction. I had very little money on hand and had to make whatever choice I made count. My Hail Mary pass was five dollar Andolini's Cash and a personal letter from me to thousands of people in a three-mile radius.

Ando Cash had our original logo in the center of a fake five dollar bill (note, be aware of counterfeit laws. Make sure your fake can't be confused with the real thing). It was good toward anything in the restaurant; I didn't care how they used it as long as they came in. In the letter, I poured my heart into explaining how much effort and thoughtfulness went into how we made everything on our menu. I emphasized that if they gave us a shot, I guaranteed they wouldn't regret it. I wanted everyone in our town to try us, and I believed that if they did, they would like us and come back. I thought I could turn people into followers once they tried us. I was right.

Notice the low resolution. Always build logos in vector. Also, make sure your discounts have an expiration date. Otherwise, you'll deal with them for going on thirteen years like me...

That worked like gangbusters, and I had swarms of people coming into my restaurant for the first time. I also realized how many ways there were to make a mistake with a successful promotion. I did put "Limit one per order," but I forgot to put an expiration date on the Ando Cash. That was 2007. People still walk in with that five-dollar-bill occasionally. But it worked. We got out of our slump; we established a new base of customers; we kept moving.

I want you to 100% know; I am not suggesting you copy that promotion verbatim. I'm saying that's what I did in 2007. I'm providing an example of an approach that worked. The world's a different place now. But the question still works, "What the hell would I do today if not one customer came in?" Would I spend a lot more money on social media? Would I make a promotional video where I speak from the heart? Would I do an email every day with a different call to action? Would I hang a sign across my neck and go up and down the street, declaring, "This is my pizza place, and I think you'll like it"? Whatever idea you answered with, that should be your newest marketing strategy. Go out, do this idea, and assess it. If it's not perfect, revise it, and do it again. Do this in the bad times, so they don't stay bad. Market this way in the good times, so people know why you're doing good. Ando Cash worked because the letter I wrote was endearing, and the call to action was a physical representation of money in their hand.

Times still get tough, marketing campaigns run their course, and great promos fade. Sometimes they fade, and you haven't even realized it. I had several promotional things going on in early 2018, but by fall, they were all failing. I needed something quick and feared going into our slow season under our projections. And then we got a gift we didn't ask for; a gift out of nowhere.

SHARE WINS HUMBLY (OR OUR TRIP ADVISOR WIN DAY)

It's October 16th, 2018. I'm driving to one of my locations in Broken Arrow. I get a text at a stoplight. It's my social media person, Meagan, who says, "Have you seen this?" I clicked the link, and I see it's a very dull press release from TripAdvisor.com. It says *"Top 10 Pizzerias in America."* I looked down to see Andolini's Pizzeria named in that list, then pulled over to process what just happened.

Here's the deal. I own a pizzeria in Tulsa, Oklahoma. In Tulsa, Oklahoma, people really like my pizza, and that's great. When I go to events or meet people from across America, and I say, "I own a pizzeria in Tulsa, Oklahoma." They say, "Tucson?" "No." "Tacoma?" "No, it's Tulsa." It's something that's always been a thorn in my side. I've lived all over America, from New York to California. I know how great Tulsa is and how much I love it. I also know how little national awareness there is for how great it is in Tulsa. It's very much like Austin was in the '90s, but without the douchebaggery or horrible traffic.

So here I am, seeing Andolini's in Tulsa, Oklahoma, recognized as one of the best-reviewed pizzerias in America. This was humbling because I realized it wasn't based on some random writer for *GQ* or *Esquire*'s opinion. This accolade wasn't what four people from the Michelin Star committee thought of us. This was purely based on the algorithm of people that had come in and reviewed Andolini's Pizzeria. The reviews are also weighted by out of town reviews, as well as the abundance of reviews received.

The other pizzerias on that list were in heavy tourism cities. Such cities as New York City, Nashville, Boston, where much of their economy is based on tourism. Reviews from tourists help a lot. Tulsa doesn't have nearly that level of tourism, but still, we made the list. I wasn't patting myself on the back at that moment. I was awestruck, and at a loss for words at how much work had gone into this moment I was totally unprepared for. I couldn't formulate how to explain to staff and my brother how big a deal this was. And oh yeah, how to emphasize enough to managers how badly our asses were going to get handed to us this weekend. The second that hits Facebook it will get on the news. Once it's on the news, we will have an increase in sales we haven't prepared for. We haven't bought enough product or scheduled enough staff. Lock and load, it's about to get nutty.

As I sent the story to my brother and other managers, the reaction was exactly what I expected it to be. Our classic Andolini's never-pat-ourselves-on-the-back response of, "They spelled this one store's name wrong." We take our humility to a fault in our approach to this business. Our ethos is to work hard, do your best, and shut up about it. Never fall in love with your bullshit and stay the course. Operationally, this mindset works well. It's not ideal for marketing.

It's good for marketing to have some humility, but you still need to market. You still must let people know your accolades, so we had to walk the line on this one. I mean, do I put a massive green banner across the restaurant saying that we're one of the best pizzerias in America based solely on reviews? Not exactly. We want people to know, but we don't want it to be the only thing they know. So, we put it out as a thank you to TripAdvisor and our customers (after all, the accolade was based on customer reviews), put a mention of it on our social pages and let it roll from there. It was the blessing that we needed to gain substantial revenue during that next slow season.

RESPOND TO REVIEWS ONLINE LIKE AN ADULT

The way we got those solid reviews is what we needed to reinvest in. If you're impressive, as we've talked about at length, to stay impressive, you need to keep on top of your presence. Not only your presence face to face with customers but your online presence as well. Whatever reviews are out there, you need to respond to and be aware of them, *you the owner*. Responding to reviews feeds the beast and keeps the review websites in your favor. Google, Yelp, TripAdvisor, and Facebook all want to reward those that actively engage in their platform. A big reason we've been well-reviewed is by consistently speaking directly to the customer. Especially when something goes wrong but also thanking them when they have a great time; if it does go wrong, we do everything to make it right, even when it means taking them to the Spite Olympics (*Callback*).

That means that if you're going to respond to reviews, you don't be a petulant child. Be kind and thankful to those that review you well. Own it for those that criticize you. Also, don't be an online jerk in general. You know what I mean... the kind of jerk who makes inappropriate remarks about people's profiles. The jerk so overtly political on Facebook you want to mute their feed. *Do not do this* when you run a business where other people's lives depend on your public perception. Heel persona or not, don't seek to piss people off about things they are emotionally invested in. Don't comment on things like religion, politics, or even sports teams. Don't touch it.

In case you take issue with that and would say the following: *"But Mike, I gotta be me. I gotta speak my mind."*

My retort: "You signed up to run a business, fuck your opinion. You represent more than yourself. You represent all those whose lives depend on your business. Make pizza, create unity, and yell your opinion into an empty coffee can, instead of a callous remark on Twitter."

AVOID FAKE ACCOLADES

We've never bought votes or made fake reviews of our stores. We've never gamed a system to win an award. It's utterly antithetical to my approach to getting them. Any distinction or website that doesn't police this becomes a hollow and fake accolade. I avoid promoting or participating in any award that isn't merit-based.

Take the Better Business Bureau, for example. The Better Business Bureau is still respected by people born before 1965. Most people born since then know that The Better Business Bureau is a sham or don't know it at all. The BBB takes in millions of dollars a year from businesses paying for their accreditation. That sticker you see at a business costs money. I have no complaints or reviews on BBB after fifteen years of business. I somehow have an A+ rating, though. It will be interesting to see if that changes a few years after this book is published. If I did get a negative review, I could pay the BBB to avoid a downgrade to my rating. I want nothing to do with this style of marketing, and neither should you. Even if you do have a geriatric following, do not compromise your values to play accolade games.

Market your wins factually from the voice of being unsolicited. I avoid being overt and seek humility in conveying a win with a more, "Hey, if you didn't know, here's something that happened," approach. It's a humblebrag, but it does work well in the discerning community. I would never market a win without representation. I would never say "Always Voted the Best," with no reference to who named us the best. No one's going to believe that accolade, and it's not even worth the price of the printing to make that sign. It's like positive movie reviews of shitty movies. If you've seen a commercial for a new movie where it shows legit reviews, you take note. If you see "*Rolling Stone* gives it five stars," and "Richard Roper says thumbs up," you'll think, "That must be a good movie." If you saw a commercial where the reviews said, "KXPS Ohio says it's a must-see." and "Plop.net calls it the best movie of the year," you know it's a con. You know this must be a pretty crappy movie. Don't do that yourself. Don't advertise a biased award. Don't announce hyperbole that has no source.

I was driving out of state and heard a radio ad that said, "If you want better Italian than us, you're never going to find it." It didn't say why or how it was the best, only this blanket statement that *you will never find anything better.* It annoyed me because it was so inauthentic. It's such a lazy way of asking people to come to try their restaurant. I hate ads like this, and I know that this type of advertising garners no real ROI. It's incredibly stupid and insulting to the customer.

I stopped into a small pizzeria in the Central Valley of California that had on their menu, "We only use the finest ingredients." Says who? What makes them fine? Are you the authority on what ingredients are officially deemed "the finest?" If they said we only use ingredients prepared in house, and all food is made to order, then that's a statement that could possibly be true. "Only the finest"—non-verifiable BS and your customer knows this. Even dumbasses know this, and if they didn't, their smart friends will influence the dumbassery, so you're not even pulling a fast one on the amateur restaurant patron.

"Only the finest" is a cliché. At one point, someone came up with it, and it was original. It became no longer original the moment someone copied it. To copy something cliched and speak in generalities is lazy. It's much more interesting to create a nuanced and detailed description. One that only pertains to your brand. To assume a generality is going resonate with anyone is foolish.

If you're the shit, you need to speak with truth to let other people in on what makes your pizzeria exceptional. If you want to advertise that you're nominated for an award in a newspaper, don't say, "Vote for us!" Say, "If you like us or want to share your opinion on other categories on this ballot, here's the poll that's going on now." It's a more subtle approach that says the same thing without being overt. If they read it and know it's from you, your customer will connect the dots.

My first award was in our small suburb location of Owasso, and we won the *Owasso Reporter* Award for Best Pizza. At the time, it was a huge deal to me. If I get an award today I didn't know we were nominated for, I stop to check myself. I call myself back to those days where we were on the edge of our seat to see if we won the Owasso Reporter Best Pizza award. I never want to take any legit accolade for granted. I want to win national awards more because that means powerful marketing fuel. That means more sales, which means more jobs and better salaries for my staff. However, any legit award deserves taking a pause to acknowledge it and gain some traction from it. Awards give us more ability to do good in our community. National awards do that easier, but never assume a small award not to be worth your time either. With Andolini's, we've always strived for excellence on par with big cities. By trying to be the best in America, I can certainly be the best in my town. If you seek only to be the best in your town, you'll never be better than that. TripAdvisor was the factual verification of that effort, and that's why it hit me so hard in a good way.

When we got the TripAdvisor award, I attributed it to my staff. It's their work and ability to execute that earned us the recognition. Because of that story, CNN, Buzzfeed, and *USA Today* all ran with that list. Food Network then named us as one of the best slices of pizza you had to try in America. We got this far by being ethical in our approach to this business. By owning up when we get it wrong and performing in a way where impressive is the goal. That approach has led us to positive reviews, and I believe it can for you as well.

But we can't rest on our laurels and say, because we won this, we're done. We're not done. We now have to keep proving every day we earned that award, and we still deserve it through our actions via food, service, and ambiance. And that's how we stay on top and continue to get awards. With that mentality and that mindset, you can do it the same. No matter what town you live in.

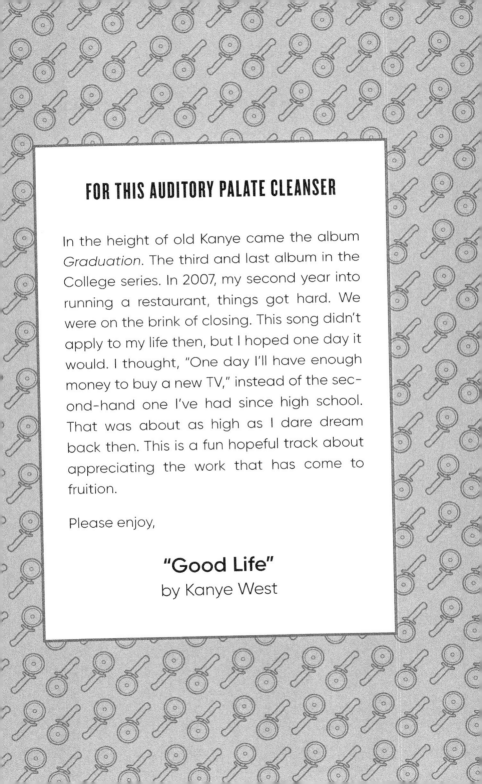

FOR THIS AUDITORY PALATE CLEANSER

In the height of old Kanye came the album *Graduation*. The third and last album in the College series. In 2007, my second year into running a restaurant, things got hard. We were on the brink of closing. This song didn't apply to my life then, but I hoped one day it would. I thought, "One day I'll have enough money to buy a new TV," instead of the second-hand one I've had since high school. That was about as high as I dare dream back then. This is a fun hopeful track about appreciating the work that has come to fruition.

Please enjoy,

"Good Life"
by Kanye West

CHAPTER 11

OWNING OWNERSHIP

Theodore Roosevelt is commonly considered the first modern president. He changed the way the presidency is viewed and made it more of a focal point than Congress. Americans chose Roosevelt the person instead of blindly choosing their parties' candidate. Roosevelt accomplished this through charisma. Roosevelt evolved presidential politics to become rooted in charisma and connection to the voter.

The presidency has molded into the acting moral compass of the nation. The president is the American CEO figurehead tasked with negotiations and dealings with other countries. They need not be a doer, but rather the visionary. Each president has done this differently, but this expectation did not exist pre-Roosevelt.

Your worth as an owner is in being the visionary of your business. In a pizzeria, it's still a requisite imperative you can toss dough and know your craft. You need to gain the respect of your staff by being able to run your line like a blue-collar worker. At the same time, never mistake that you, the owner, are in a white-collar executive position. If you don't act as a visionary and lead, you're just a glorified employee.

You have a fantastic amount of opportunity in front of you. Not only to guide the culture of your local community but also to directly affect lives. You get to be the boss that you always wanted. That should be your approach. Does that matter to you? Of course, it does. For any charity and outreach you give, you get to choose it. No one's forcing you to help some crappy corporate shill of a charity. You know the kind, the ones large corporations choose because it's an easy write-off. No, you can select a charity that's moving the needle in your community. You get to make a choice that matters.

You can be the one who truly helps others in your town. You can be the person that actually makes your world a better place. You get to help guide your employees' views on what an ethical business is. You can be the person that your staff trusts, rather than the person that your staff dreads.

All your preconceived notions of what a leader and visionary are need to be reevaluated. Being simply "a boss" is underselling the value of your position. You are the face of your company. As the spokesperson for your brand, you not only help your marketing, you also increase your worth as an individual. Being the face doesn't mean you have to be Mr. Gorgeous. It does mean that you live your brand.

Wendy's brand's spokesperson was Dave Thomas, and he lived his brand. His basic approach of speaking directly to the camera in commercials resonated. His endearing quality took Wendy's to new heights for decades. At first, he was criticized for being stiff on camera. But the reality approach of the real founder talking about his product worked. Dave's authenticity was ahead of its time. In today's world, authenticity in the story is what people crave more than ever, a true story from a genuine owner. It is why people watch *Shark Tank* and root for the earnest people giving their pitch who have a story to tell.

To be the visionary means you look to the future. Ask yourself, "What else can we add?" and "What existing things do we need to change or enhance?" That includes staff; what is your plan to keep each employee growing in your business? That takes vision, not kicking the can down the road or the mindset of another day another dollar. Yes, you are responsible for creating a vision for your staff as well.

Tending to other people's futures might be a weird concept to you. If you've always worried about yourself and let others do their thing, this won't be in your wheelhouse. It wasn't in my wheelhouse when I started at twenty-two. But people will hang on your every word when you pay them. Imagine telling an employee's family members how important they are to the place they work. That wouldn't matter if you weren't their boss; because you are their leader, it holds weight and matters. When you're their boss, their authority figure, you now have a power you might not have felt you signed up for. But it's there. And it's your duty and responsibility to take it very seriously. That means you nurture their growth as their leader instead of being another lackluster boss or, worse, being perceived as only a coworker.

It doesn't mean you're a know-it-all mapping out staffs' personal lives. It doesn't mean that for every question that ever gets asked, you have to have the answer. It means that you have to dedicate yourself to listening to your staff. It means for any answer you don't know you seek to find it out. It also means you get to have fun and be creative with what you do with your vision.

You get to add all the nuances that make your brand profitable, to help provide for your staff. Creative thinking gets to be a large part of your job. You get to name all the food items and actualize your vision. Naming things uniquely helps you stand out. Even super corporate Taco Bell seeks to be unique and stand out. They created the Loaded Griller instead of naming it a burrito and the Crunchwrap instead of "taco sandwich." Big money marketing knows to make things different and unlike another restaurant's menu. If your Caprese antipasto is the (blank) Caprese antipasto, it's now less comparable to someone else's basic Caprese. That's one quick adjustment of a food item that made it a little more unique to you. That is your duty and responsibility as an owner. It's your job to create as unique an experience as possible.

It's your duty to create systems. You must not be the cog but rather the brain. It's on you to come up with solutions and resources for things you don't know how to do yourself or figure a way to gain that knowledge. You don't have shackles on your effort; no one is going to tell you not to try something. However, that requires you to be the self-starter visionary your business needs.

ETHICAL OWNERSHIP

Being the ethical leader of your business is paramount to your success. What ethics? I am not demanding you become a saint or adopt a religion if you're an atheist. I am only encouraging you to be a decent human who is law-abiding and cares about your community. I am telling you to be exceptionally quality-focused and family-focused if you want success. No matter your brand, your food is made and served by people with families and people who want to be a part of something great. If that's not at the forefront of your brand, then your brand is weak.

Having integrity and morals in how you pay staff keeps them trusting you. Paying the compliance licenses, service fees, vendors, and all your bills on time is how you maintain your moral standing in the community. If you don't pay on time, never expect any of the people you slow pay to go to bat for you when the chips are down. *FYI, the chips will inevitably be down at some point.*

MORALE OWNERSHIP

For new employees, do you say, "Hey, how are you? What's your name? Where'd you work before you worked here? How do you like it so far?" Sometimes, I crack jokes. For example, I'll say to a new manager, "Hey, who do you want me to fire today?" I say it with a healthy level of sarcasm because that would never actually occur, but I break the ice and show I'm a human.

Become a great gift-giver to make an impact on your staff's morale. You can always give a raise additionally, but a gift shows you notice their effort. Find out music an employee is into then trade out some pizzas for concert tickets. Say, "I know (blank band) is in town, here's two tickets and I already made sure you got the night off. Thank you for all that you do here." The impact of that gesture turns an employee into a disciple. It goes beyond praise.

Whenever you meet an employee's family member, let them know how valuable they are to your restaurant. If you're speaking to an employee's child, say, "Hey, it's because of your (mother/father) that our business runs as well as it does." That'll matter more than complimenting the individual with no one else there. It matters because it pulls to their other life, their home life. This job provides for that home life but also takes them away from that home life. Let the family know as much as possible that the time they aren't home matters to the other people they are around.

To parents of my high school kids, I say, "Hey, just so you know, your kid's not only a terrific kid, but they also have a great future because of (X and Y reason)." Don't lie but dig down deep into your feelings and your appreciation for that employee, and share it with that employee's direct home life. You'll reinforce your bond with that employee and strengthen their home life's relationship with your business. These actions can be the deciding factor between staying at your job or going to a new one when life issues come into play.

HOW DO YOU PERCEIVE YOURSELF AS AN OWNER?

My wife works for the real estate agency Keller Williams Realty. Gary Keller, owner of Keller Williams, has some important words he uses with his leadership team. He says, "Be very careful how you view yourself." The reason why? The way you view yourself is likely different from how your staff sees you. And how they see you matters because perception is nine-tenths of reality. You need to learn whatever their perception is, and either reinforce it or change it to what you want it to be.

Everything you put out there will affect your perception. You'll need to be "*on*" every time you are in front of employees. Having a Resting Bitch Face (RBF), i.e., being a sour puss or looking like one, can negatively affect your ability to lead. Walking into your store like a bull in a china shop who only points out what is wrong will hurt your ability to lead. When you enter your store as an owner, know that you are on stage performing for your staff. Grow morale and goodwill before tending to tiny issues.

WELL-ROUNDED OWNERSHIP

Learn your whole store, not just the role you are most comfortable performing. If you're a food-centric owner who's all about the pizza, switch it up. Go into the front of your restaurant, be around customers more, be an owner to your whole team, not only your niche. If you're a gadfly but aren't comfortable in a kitchen, change it up and work the line.

Staff must see you in every position, from the top down, so they know you are everyone's leader. They must know this owner is not only an owner to one segment of the restaurant's staff. Do this to earn respect and also give respect back to your staff as a reliable operational worker with them. You're not doing this because you're needed to work the oven. You do this to be more well-rounded and increase staff morale.

SYSTEM HEALTH OWNERSHIP

You must hold people accountable and maintain the systems you've created. Remember that *inspection*, not *expectation*, is the only way systems remain effective and operational. Keep your staff using and abiding by the systems. Hold staff to the standard and not the other way around. Drill this into your head as your operational mandate. Then drill that into your workforce.

Maintain the financial health of your restaurant by reevaluating your contracts every year. Accomplish this via your calendar system. Keep your own systems, the ones that you are personally responsible for doing, inspected by you, or have a check that calls you out if you ever slip on doing your role.

KILL YOUR EGO

Your ego is not your friend. Being self-deprecating can increase the morale of a restaurant and your worth as an owner. Great actors work to make the movie better, not just how they come off. When a serious actor commits hard to a comedic role that makes them look foolish, you know they're a pro. They would do anything for the story, or in our world, the business. As a result, the story worked, and they looked better for it. You have to be willing to sacrifice your ego to gain the greater good.

When my staff put a goofy photo of me in high school up on the bar, I didn't take it down. It was fun. I got the joke. And I left it there. When people say, "That was a horrible Hawaiian shirt you had in high school." I come back with, "And I still have it, and I would still wear it tomorrow." I don't say, "Yeah, take that down," or, "Who said you could put that up there?" I don't do that because it's not good for morale, and lousy morale is bad for business.

BRAND PRESERVATION

Another aspect of your worth as an owner is maintaining your restaurant brand. Things that could hurt your restaurant's brand, you must do away with. If someone comes in and says, "Hey, we want to put a gumball machine near the front door of your restaurant. It'll give you a few bucks a month. And why not? Kids love it." Your natural inclination could be, "Yeah, OK, sure." The problem with that is, you don't sell gumballs. You sell pizza. And now this is a distraction from that. Your new brand involves a gumball machine as the first or last thing your customer sees when they walk in. You should not allow gumball or candy machines in the front of your restaurant. Don't allow in anything that distracts from your brand and confuses your message.

It's a very base example, but it relates to everything else you do and the choices you make for your restaurant.

Don't put ads on your menu for other businesses. It doesn't matter that it'll reduce your menu cost, it's a shortsighted move. Unless it's on par with all revenue you will take in, it's a distraction. Don't compromise your direct communication with the customer as a way to save on printing costs. It dilutes your message.

When you first open a restaurant, you're on the bottom survival level of Maslow's hierarchy of needs. The goal is to get to the self-actualization level at the top where you're making an impact. To get there, you need to gain stability. After that, the goal is appreciation. Then on the hierarchy, the goal moves to earning the respect of your community. Once all those are set, you self-actualize affecting your world. It's entirely possible to get to that point. And that is, again, your worth as an owner.

You are an owner, not a CEO. You're not a chief executive officer. You're an owner-operator of a pizzeria. Don't ever let the ego bullshit of a corner office get in the way of your ability to lead your staff to higher goals.

MR. RINALDI: THE FIRST GREAT OWNER I MET

I rode the bus as a kid. I had to walk to a bus stop and take the bus. A few of the bus drivers had kind attitudes; some not as pleasant. Then one day, there was a new guy driving the bus. He was easily the nicest person I had ever met in my life. He asked how every single kid was doing. He listened. Put in funny quips and stories of himself. And genuinely seemed like the best, most charismatic individual I had ever met.

I was thinking to myself, "How is this guy a bus driver?" I was only ten years old, but it didn't check out; he was too into his job. It turns out his name was the name of the bus company. Rinaldi. That was Mr. Rinaldi. Mr. Rinaldi decided that he wanted to take a bus route now and again. He wanted to be boots on the ground to see how the kids were doing. He wanted to see if he noticed any issues with the routes. He also wanted to show his staff he could still hang and drive a bus route.

Everything about that experience taught me what I wanted to be. I wanted to own something, and I wanted to know how it worked. Mr. Rinaldi was the exemplification of that. A guy who owned his business loved what he did and did it well. Again, a regular old bus driver, but I still remember it almost thirty years later. The experience I had with him lasted. That's the impact you can have in your pizzeria because your pizzeria is more than just a pizzeria.

OWN YOUR ROLE AND BE PRESENT

Don't treat your staff like automatons. Don't act like a rich asshole because you can't afford to be an asshole.

OWNING OWNERSHIP · 263

You're a member of a team. Not only that, you're also the leader of that team. You need to work on your business and not work in your business. You still need to be in your business daily to impact these changes. As you grow, that gets harder and harder. My workaround has been to create a training program based on videos. This way, I am the one personally training the new hire like they're right next to me. It's more impersonal than actually being there but better than not working with me at all.

I show my personality and my belief structure off in these videos. I speak in a non-corporate robot way, so they know our style. I've done these videos with my brother, so that they, the average employee, knows who we are and what we stand for. So, that way, they can mirror it and not have an ambiguous feeling about what the goal of this business is.

BECOMING AND REMAINING UNSLICED

I have to stop and think to myself, how did I get here? Not in a melancholy way but more fascination with the randomness of life. It doesn't make a ton of sense. By now, I'm supposed to be a former JAG lawyer who's working at some law firm in San Francisco. Instead, I'm in Tulsa, Oklahoma, with three-hundred-plus employees, running a pizza restaurant. If you want to tell God a joke, tell him your plans.

My "joke" has become something that has benefited hundreds of families and mine, and their families,
and their family's families. It's not a joke at all. It's an
unplanned path that has resulted in fifteen-plus years
of business. And it's something that I know happened
for a reason.

Whether you believe in fate is irrelevant. The fact is
these things happened and I'm happy they did. You can
be successful as well and do these things for yourself.

It's hard not to get sliced up by this business. You
must remain whole: with those closest to you, with
your values intact, and with your bank account growing
instead of shrinking. To be Unsliced means your community worth increases as your worries decrease.

To remain or become Unsliced means you trust
and believe not only in yourself but also in your staff.
Your worth goes beyond your value alone. When you're
Unsliced, you also help those you've provided for bring
their own value to the work. *Because of your influence,
they can also give greatness to the world.*

That's the *Unsliced* mantra.

FOR THIS FINAL AUDITORY PALATE CLEANSER

Whole books could be written about this song. The final track off *Revolver* was the first song recorded for the album. It was conceptualized during the Rubber Soul sessions as an existential song. It's a song that took on all clichés of songwriting and, in its effort, created song sampling. A technique that would become the bedrock of rap music and most new music today. The Beatles took every skill that had led them to this point, to boldly create something completely different. The title is never spoken in the song, but the song emits a feeling as if that's all that is said. We don't know what tomorrow will bring, but we know we will use the skills that have gotten us to this point. The next goal is to use them then to do something we've never done before. This equals perpetual growth.

Please enjoy,

"Tomorrow Never Knows"
by The Beatles

STAYING RELEVANT

GOING FOR THE "NEXT, NEXT THING" AND BEING REGIS PHILBIN

When we opened Andolini's Pizzeria, I was twenty-two years old. My goal was to make the best possible product I could and let everything else fall into place. I wanted to enhance the lives of everyone involved by making Andolini's the go-to spot for friends and family. It was—and remains—an altruistic but straightforward goal. Back then, youth was on my side, and I had fresh eyes for this business. My eyes may have been dumb, naive, and not very self-aware, but they were fresh.

The business is now woven into the fabric of Tulsa. That's something I take a lot of pride in. As time moves on, my goals have shifted. I want Andolini's to not only be a part of the culture but also help develop the future of Tulsa's culture. That might sound grandiose coming from an average pizza guy, but it's important to me and should be relevant to all businesses. If you want to continue to grow, you have to seek to impact the next generation. At Andolini's, we don't define our success by our achievements but rather by our ability to affect and influence. The current goal is to continually hit the "Next, Next Thing:" the something that no one else is touching yet, which means you can lead the pack, be first to market, and define the perception. Don't just rest on your previous success. Don't even go after the next big thing that the guy around the way is already doing. In my eyes, we should have already seen it if it's just the next big thing. Again, I want the Next, *Next*. I also don't want to do the new thing for the sake of it; I want to do it the best. That's the promise we are delivering to the customer, that if we come out with something, it's going to be vetted.

Our success is not defined by my brother or me. Our success comes from our focus on developing the next round of pizza makers and business-minded people. Those people, those Type A people, want to be a part of pioneering the industry, not following trends. Any business predicated upon one person is only as good as that one person. It's thereby destined to fail when that one person can no longer do what they do.

That's why writing off the next generation as "less than my generation" is dumb. It's human nature to do so, but it's still dumb. It's akin to ten-year-old fifth graders looking down on nine-year-old fourth graders. Imagine those kids at recess saying, "Back when I was in fourth grade, we knew what cool was. These new kids are into reading *The Boxcar Children*. When we were rocking fourth grade, it was *Hardy Boys* all day."

It's an old-fashioned business attitude to be "too cool" or "unimpressed" by the new school. But the ability to take what you've learned and give it to someone else is legacy building. This way, they grow and learn from you, and your legacy lives on. At the same time, being older does not make you the arbiter of knowledge. Being able to learn from someone younger and utilize their fresh perspective makes both parties stronger. The younger generation can look at the past as history rather than be tied to it emotionally as a memory. This means they have a different, underutilized perspective. It can give them a more unbiased outlook than you have on the same situation. Remember that the enemy of tomorrow is the complacency of today. Integrating young and old perspectives are how businesses must function to stay relevant. I not only trust all of my staff members to be a part of our vision but also to help me mold it. Whatever age they are is an opportunity.

A year is not that much time in the grand scheme of existence. It's smaller than a minuscule blip in the history of the earth. Fifteen years have gone by like nothing. When I look back to 2005, I like all the same bands I do today. *Saturday Night Live* has some of the same cast members still on the show today. My personality hasn't changed much at all. Fifteen years ago, I had already graduated from college and started Andolini's.

Then I ponder all the changes that have occurred in the last fifteen years. In fifteen years, we've had three presidents, the invention of social media, and the introduction of the smartphone. In reality, a ton has changed, and fifteen years is a *long* time. Not just in technology but the way the world works. Regarding fifteen-year spurts of change, think how much happened from 1959 to 1974. In 1959, TV still broadcast in black and white; no one had ever heard of the Beatles. By 1974, the Beatles had created every album they would ever make and broken up. All the while, we landed on the moon and had five different presidents. Eisenhower, JFK, Johnson, Nixon, and Ford. Fifteen years is a long, long time in terms of culture. Today is moving faster than time progressed in the 1960s; today we're moving at a breakneck speed.

It's easy to think that once you've got your finger on the pulse of what's happening, then you're set and that that's the way it'll always be. I wish it were true, but it simply is not. There are about ten pizzerias in America that can still pull off a cash-only system, like it's 1974. If you can and still make a profit doing that, good for you. Odds are you can't. Any pizzeria that's not rolling in cash and still isn't taking plastic is a dinosaur, and dinosaurs go extinct. Old school pizzeria culture is aging out. Marketable nostalgia lasts through one new generation, two at best. In 1994, college kids wanted to relive the Woodstock of their parents from 1969. By the 2000s, *That 70's Show* became popular on TV. In the 2010s, *The Goldberg's* and *Stranger Things* became popular, reflecting on the 1980s. As 2020 begins, I'm seeing kids in Nirvana shirts and fanny packs back in style as the 1990s nostalgia wave begins. Nostalgia has a twenty-five- to-forty-year cap on marketability.

The debate to accept credit cards was an issue of fifteen years ago. It's not a debate anymore. The problem of today is the operator who doesn't believe social media is relevant—the owner who is living off nostalgia and not seeking relevance. The pizzeria not engaged in learning everything there is to know about Instagram. Most every pizzeria owner gets that they should have a Facebook page. Several still don't go all in to understand the metrics of how to maximize Facebook and every other platform. Your marketing decisions are as vital as your choice of flour. Not knowing how or why you do things on social media is like not knowing your brand of flour. It truly is that big of a deal now and staying relevant is understanding social media. Seek relevance everywhere, your POS choice, food developments, uniforms, ambiance, everything.

My motto for staying relevant is "Be Regis." Be Regis Philbin. Here's a guy, who into his late 80s, was still on live TV talking about hitting the town the night before with his wife, Joy. He would then talk about what he tweeted today and why he loves today's guest of the show. Typically, the guest was a new actor or a young recording artist. Regis got his start in the '50s on NBC and could hold his own on any talk show until the day he passed. He was forced to retire from *Regis and Kelly*, but he was still engaged and knew about the "newest thing" until his last day on air. He never looked down on the next wave but instead found a way to ride it. When he finally passed at age eighty-eight, I was caught off guard; I figured he had another decade in him. Imagine that, an eighty-eight-year-old man's death felt untimely. That's because his vitality was directly linked to his dedication to remaining relevant.

It's very flippant for someone over the age of thirty to write off social media. It's even easier for someone in their forties or fifties to say, "Instagram is not for me; I don't understand that stuff." To those who act this way, heed this warning: you are knowledgeably making a business mistake. Time will kick your ass unless you stay relevant and *be Regis*. That means not only seeking to follow trends but also making them your own. No one says you have to use Instagram the same way as someone who is twenty. Do it your way, learn it, get better, and do it often.

Today, effectively keeping your business relevant has nothing to do with the Yellow Pages. The tools that worked before 2007 are not useful anymore. If your pizzeria is over a decade old and you're over the age of thirty-five, you must act differently than you did then. The beauty of understanding you might not be great at something means you're on the path to the best way to fix it. So today, start with your social media presence.

I didn't write this book to bloviate or give advice because I'm special. I genuinely feared the future and lived in a constant state of panic for years, not knowing if things would be OK. These lessons got me to a place where it's better than OK; it's thriving. Now I want to share these lessons with you, in case you're still in a place of fear. This book was written to that owner, the one in that uneasy place. I wrote this for you. To the owner who is out of that funk now and doing OK, I wrote this for you to question what next things you can take on, just like I do myself.

Here is an unabashed and declarative thank you for reading this along with a war cry to dig deep and push this industry forward. Do something new and different, challenge me so my team and I can challenge you. Pizza is unique and different from other food; you already know that. Now is the time to lead. Now is the time to go after that Next Next, to make lives better via cheese on bread.

AND NOW...THE ESSENTIAL BOH PLAYLIST TO GET SHIT DONE QUICK AND KEEP MORALE HIGH

Please enjoy,

1. **Through the Fire and Flames** by DragonForce
2. **7 Words** by Deftones
3. **Don't Need It** by Bad Brains
4. **Good as Hell** by Lizzo
5. **The Bitter End** by Sum 41
6. **Rock Star** by N.E.R.D.
7. **Drop It Low** by Ester Dean
8. **The Suit** by Domeshots
9. **Yeah!** by Usher featuring Lil' Jon & Ludacris
10. **Phoebe Cates** by Fenix TX
11. **Sabotage** by Beastie Boys
12. **Blitzkrieg Bop** by The Ramones
13. **Come Sail Away** (144 BPM Remix) by STYX
14. **Rump Shaker** by Wreckx-N-Effect
15. **Engine No. 9** by Deftones
16. **Numb/Encore** by Jay-Z & Linkin Park
17. **Familiar** by Incubus
18. **Break it Down (DX Entrance Song)** by Chris Warren Band

19. **I'm The Man (Def Uncensored Version)** by Anthrax
20. **Bootylicious** by Destiny's Child
21. **She Caught The Katy** by The Blues Brothers
22. **Through The Wire** by Kanye West
23. **It's Goin' Down** by X-Ecutioners
24. **Shake Ya Tailfeather** by Nelly, P. Diddy, Murphy Lee
25. **Work It** by Missy Elliot
26. **Bad Reputation** by Thin Lizzy
27. **Light 'Em Up** by Fall Out Boy
28. **Death Or Glory** by Social Distortion
29. **Dyers Eve** by Metallica
30. **B.O.B.** by Outkast
31. **Transformer** by Gnarls Barkley
32. **Gonna Make You Sweat (Everybody Dance Now)** by C+C Music Factory
33. **Bizarre Love Triangle** by New Order
34. **Bop Gun (One Nation)** by Ice Cube
35. **Planet Rock [Swordfish Mix]** by Paul Oakenfold
36. **Peter Piper** by Run-D.M.C.
37. **A Favor House Atlantic** by Coheed & Cambria
38. **Super Bass** by Nikki Minaj
39. **Big Take Over** by Bad Brains

40. **Baby Got Back** by Sir Mix-A-Lot

41. **Get Low** by Lil John

42. **Let's Bash** by The Lonely Island

43. **It Takes Two** by Rob Base & DJ E-Z Rock

44. **Rhyme Stealer** by Sugar Ray

45. **I'm OK, You're OK** by MxPx

46. **Miles Away** by Goldfinger

47. **My Best Friend** by Weezer

48. **Turn Down for What** by DJ Snake & Lil Jon

49. **Party Hard** by Andrew W.K.

50. **Bantamburgh** by Salmon

51. **When the Last Time** by Clipse

52. **Just A Friend** by Biz Markie

53. **Rapper's Delight** by Erick Sermon

54. **Radio Cambodia** by Glassjaw

55. **88** by Sum 41

56. **Ms. New Booty** by Bubba Sparxxx

57. **Banned In The U.S.A.** by 2 Live Crew

58. **Dance (A$$)** by Big Sean

59. **You're The Best** by Joe 'Bean' Eposito

60. **Children Of The Revolution** by T.Rex

61. **Halloween** by Helloween

62. **Time** by Zebrahead

63. **White Man In Hammersmith Palais** by 311

64. **Ms. Doorbell (The White Stripes + Mos Def)** by Adrian Champion

65. **The Spirit of Radio** by Rush
66. **Wicked** by Korn
67. **Low (feat. T-Pain)** by Flo Rida
68. **Protect Ya Neck (Shao Lin Version)** by Wu-Tang Clan
69. **On My Own (feat. Corey Taylor)** by Travis Barker
70. **Trying To Find A Balance** by Atmosphere
71. **Rise Above** by Black Flag
72. **Lean On Sheena** by Avoid One Thing
73. **Blood Red Summer** by Coheed & Cambria
74. **Oh No** by Girl Talk
75. **Ditty** by Paperboy
76. **Renegades Of Funk** by Rage Against The Machine
77. **Da Rockwilder** by Method Man & Redman
78. **Bleed It Out** by Linkin Park
79. **Galaxy** by Hot Sauce Johnson
80. **Anaconda** by Nicki Minaj
81. **Faint** by Linkin Park
82. **Got Your Money (feat. Kelis)** by Ol' Dirty Bastard
83. **Movies** by Alien Ant Farm
84. **New Skin** by Incubus

85. **Wu-Tang Clan Aint Nuthing ta F' Wit** by Wu-Tang Clan
86. **Distortion** by Rev Run
87. **Patience Is A Virtue** by Normal Like You
88. **Stone Cold Crazy** by Metallica
89. **Homebrew (2004)** by 311
90. **Build Me Up Buttercup** by The Goops
91. **Alive** by Pearl Jam
92. **Susanne** by Weezer
93. **Never Ending Story Theme Song** by A New Found Glory
94. **Abba Zabba** by Fenix TX
95. **Same Old Song** by Sev
96. **In Da Club** by 50 Cent
97. **Superman** by Goldfinger
98. **Dirt Off Your Shoulder** by Jay-Z
99. **Wanna Be Startin'/Seven Nation Army** by TRV$ DJ-AM
100. **Mind On The Road** by Rev Run

UNSLICED RESTAURANT TERMS GLOSSARY

86'd: When an item is out of stock or unavailable

BBB: The Better Business Bureau (a crap organization that sells a paid-for accreditation)

BIB: Bag in a Box soda syrup

BLP: Basic Leadership Plan

BOH: Back of House/Kitchen staff

Cousin Oliver: When someone shows up unexpectedly and is out of place like Cousin Oliver on the fifth and final season of The Brady Bunch. Example: "We have a packed house, and I got a Cousin Oliver throwing dough who has never tossed dough in their life on display and has no business doing so."

D1M: Day 1 Mentality

DIY: Do It Yourself

DRI: Directly Responsible Individual

EXPO: Expediter or Food Runner tasked with running a restaurant's ticket board

FOGO DI CHOW: Acceptable non-curse word or phrase you can use in supplementation of curse words when in a public setting. Example: "They can go Fogo Di Chow themselves." Or "This Fogo Di Chow is getting old quick."

FOH: Front of house/Servers

GDP: Gross Domestic Product

GM: General Manager

GSD: Get shit done

GTG: Good to Go (sometimes abbreviated as G2G)

G4U: Good for You (always said with condescension)

IM3: *Iron Man 3* or something that seems good at the start but has no meaning or consequence, like at the end of *Iron Man 3* when Tony Stark destroys all the Iron Man suits and retires as Iron Man only to have all the suits again at the beginning of his next MCU appearance in *Avengers Age of Ultron* inexplicably. Example: *"So Shelia IM3'd us last night, she said she was short on cash this week and asked to pick up shifts but just released her prime Friday night bar shift."*

JORTS: Jean Shorts. Typically worn by children in the 1990s whose mothers didn't want to buy new clothes in the summer and just hemmed their winter jeans

KM: Kitchen Manager

KID: Anyone you are responsible for

LDP: Lou Diamond Phillips (who has made zero contributions to this book)

MOD: Manager on Duty

MTM: Manager Training Meeting

OCS: Officer Candidate School

RBF: Resting Bitch Face

SEO: Search Engine Optimization

SOP: Standard Operating Procedure

SWAGU: The liquid form of swag or swagger (commonly aligned with swagger sauce or Zima)

TLA: Three Letter Acronym

UNFUCK: The art of taking a perplexing, disastrous, and/or detrimental situation and course correcting it via ingenuity and spiteful resolve

USP: Unique Selling Point

USMC: United States Marine Corps

WCDT: We Can Do That (because fuck yeah, we can)

ABOUT THE AUTHOR

Mike Bausch is an industry leader whose restaurant, Andolini's Pizzeria, is a top ten pizzeria in the US, as named by TripAdvisor, BuzzFeed, CNN, and *USA Today*. Andolini's began in 2005 and has grown to five pizzerias, two gelaterias, two food-hall concepts, a food truck, and a fine-dining restaurant by 2019. Mike is a World Pizza Champion, a Guinness Book world record holder, and a writer for *Pizza Today*.

Mike is part of a Marine Corps family who has lived across America from New York to California. Mike calls Tulsa home and lives with his wife, Michelle, and son, Henry.

For more information, questions,
speaking, and inquires visit
www.UnslicedBook.com.

Printed in Great Britain
by Amazon